D0559941

NEW THEMES
IN WESTERN CANADIAN GEOGRAPHY:
THE LANGARA PAPERS

B.C. GEOGRAPHICAL SERIES, NUMBER 22

OCCASIONAL PAPERS IN GEOGRAPHY

Edited by
BRENTON M. BARR, Ph.D.

Department of Geography
The University of Calgary

WITHDRAWN
☐ DESELECTED
☐ LOST
☐ DAMAGED
☐ MISSING (INV.)
☐ OTHER

Published with the assistance of

THE SENATOR NORMAN M. PATERSON FOUNDATION

Tantalus Research Limited

Publisher - Vancouver, Canada

B.C. GEOGRAPHICAL SERIES, NUMBER 22

Editorial Address:
W.G. Hardwick, Ph.D.
Department of Geography
The University of British Columbia
2075 Wesbrook Place
Vancouver, B.C., V6T 1W5

Circulation Address:
B.C. Geographical Series
P.O. Box 34248
2405 Pine Street
Vancouver, B.C., V6J 4N8

STANDARD BOOK NUMBER 0-919-478-34-4
CN-ISSN 0068-1571
COPYRIGHT © 1976 Tantalus Research Limited

Canadian Cataloguing in Publication Data

Main entry under title:

New themes in Western Canadian geography

(B.C. geographical series ; no. 22) (Occasional papers in geography)

"Some papers presented at the annual meeting of the Western Division, Canadian Association of Geographers, March 1975."
ISBN 0-919478-34-4 pa.

1. Anthropo-geography — Addresses, essays, lectures. 2. Geography — Addresses, essays, lectures. I. Barr, Brenton M., 1940- II. Canadian Association of Geographers. Western Division. III. Series. IV. Series.
GF8.N49   910   C76-016007-4

® T.M. Reg. Canada 1973

B.C. Geographical Series © 1966, Tantalus Research Limited

PRINTED IN CANADA

by

CAMPBELL PRINTING LTD.

TABLE OF CONTENTS

SPECIAL ACKNOWLEDGMENT

This is the third of four possible volumes
of "Occasional Papers in Geography" to be
published with financial assistance from
Senator Norman M. Paterson. The Editor,
and the Western Division Executive, are
grateful to Senator Paterson for his en-
couragement and support of this western
Canadian geographical journal.

INTRODUCTION

Brenton M. Barr
The University of Calgary

This volume contains some of the papers presented at the
Annual Meeting of the Western Division, Canadian Association of
Geographers, held at Vancouver City College, Vancouver, B.C., in
March, 1975. "Occasional Papers in Geography" is published with the
assistance of an Editorial Board consisting of experienced members
of the Western Division who are active in Alberta, British Columbia,
or Washington State. Each manuscript submitted to the Editor was
read by the Editor, the Chairman of the Editorial Board, a member of
the Editorial Board, and at least two referees selected by a member
of the Editorial Board. The Editorial Board and the Editor attempt
to ensure that the articles published in this volume meet the requirements of scholarship; but they are also sensitive to the role
of the Western Division in promotion of academic research, in en-
couragement of graduate students and "neophytes," in exploration of
the relationship of geography to teaching and education, and in
development of an important publication of research studies in the
area served by the Western Division.

The twelve articles in this volume relate to research in
human and physical geography although the major research emphasis of
ten papers focuses on aspects of human geography.

This volume of "Occasional Papers in Geography" commences
with a paper originally presented at the annual banquet of the Division by Dean Scarfe of The University of British Columbia who examines some of the key publications in recent North American and
British geographical literature for trends and portents of what lies
ahead for geography in this decade of change and intellectual fer-
ment. Dean Scarfe suggests that, in the 1970's, "good Geography is
coming back into its own . . . we are again looking at the real landscape but more closely and critically than before." He suggests that,
although geography is a broad discipline, the major characteristic of
geographers throughout the field is increasingly one of basing theory

on initial exploratory practical work and a movement away from an excessive dependence on *a priori* reasoning devoid of real-world experience. Through their mounting concern for the safety and survival of man's total environment, geographers dealing with physical and human aspects of the world are viewing their endeavours as increasingly interdependent.

The interdependency of human and physical environments is stressed in this volume by many geographers such as John Chapman in his consideration of "Geographers and Energy." "Energetics"--the energy inputs, transformations and outputs of identified systems-- has recently started to diffuse into geography; Chapman's prime concern is with the impact this diffusion has had on the field of economic geography and with the validity of the claim that "energetics" is a unifying force between the sub-disciplines of physical and human geography. Chapman concludes that "energetics" offers considerable potential for "fruitful research and innovative teaching . . . to foster cohesion between physical and human geographers," although he appears rather disappointed with the progress to date in the incorporation of "energetics" into the spatial analyses and modelling exercises of economic geographers.

The one paper in this volume related to the geography of transport deals with the application of graph-theoretic measures to the growth of the Alberta highway network. These measures permit evaluation and description of the topological complexities of networks and have been applied by Monanu and Hodgson to evaluate the developing complexity of the Alberta highway network over time, i.e., 1934-1974. Their study provides both a certain amount of empirical information and an evaluation of the utility and meaning of graph-theoretic measures, although the authors caution that there exists a danger "of imputing too much importance to them as indicators of economic development." More investigation into this problem is both required and, in the authors' view, warranted.

The only other paper in this volume dealing with Alberta is an investigation of inter-industry manufacturing linkages by Barr and Fairbairn. These authors investigate the number and value of backward and forward inter-industry manufacturing linkages of 503 establishments in Alberta, approximately one-quarter of all those manufacturing establishments operating in 1972. They also investigate the extent to which manufacturers buy and sell to other manufacturers in their same industrial group. Their analysis, part of a major investigation into spatial industrial complexity in Alberta, concludes that provincial manufacturers have numerous but weak backward manufacturing ties within Alberta but have sizeable although relatively less numerous forward linkages with manufacturers. Alberta manufacturers are important suppliers of provincial demand for manufactured goods but also ship a large proportion of their output beyond provincial boundaries. In terms of inter-industry

absorption of manufactured commodities, the only recognizable industrial complexes--although still weakly developed--in Alberta are
related to the food and beverage, and to the primary metal, engineering, and transportation equipment industries.

Two papers in this volume deal with spatial conflict; both
analyze issues which have developed recently in the lower mainland
region of British Columbia. J. Bradbury examines the expansion of
an oil refinery in Greater Vancouver to provide a case study to
illustrate both the unequal competition between interested bodies
and the many factors involved in any one landuse conflict. Of the
three main groups involved in the conflict--the Chevron Oil Company,
the Burnaby Municipal Council, and the Burnaby Concerned Citizens--
the oil company won and the citizens lost. The Municipal Council
apparently never felt its position particularly threatened or the
issue worthy of serious consideration by politicians. The other
conflict documented in this volume--the general problem of social,
economic, and political viability of Point Roberts, Washington State,
although generating large expenditures of time and money by local,
regional and national authorities--has not been resolved and appears
now to be in a state of limbo although the passions which led to the
investigation documented by Manfred Vernon are likely to be aroused
again if any one of the groups involved should appear to gain an
advantage in realizing its objectives. Both these studies demonstrate the increasing concern by different interest groups to ensure that change in landuse does not proceed without challenge in
those areas where many facets of the public interest are at stake.

Three studies in this collection investigate attitudes of
and perception by, environmental participants in order to expand
the geographer's awareness of the role played by these concepts in
spatial research. D. Porteous suggests that geographers should
venture into the realm of microspace to analyze differences in environmental preference and adaption. P. Murphy and L. Halliday
suggest that geography has become a study of the adult world and
has not paid sufficient attention to the needs and interests of
youth or the elderly; their paper discusses the degree to which
children's perceptions of local parks are in harmony with the official policies underlying development of the parks, and the authors
conclude that "children do not perceive and use their neighbourhood
parks in the way envisioned or planned by the local municipality."
Although they do not carry their investigation further, the authors
do suggest that such divergent views ultimately bear the seeds of
conflict among spatial users and designers. The notion of spatial
perception and adaption by spatial users to resolve movement problems
during religious pilgrimages is investigated by H. Tanaka who discusses in his paper the way in which religious merit and convenience
are at least partially accommodated through spatial temporal adjustment. These three papers, by drawing evidence from culturally diverse regions of the world, seem to bear out Dean Scarfe's observa-

tions in the initial paper in this volume that human and physical interaction are increasingly becoming important research topics after many decades of neglect by geographers.

Environmental adaption by groups rather than individuals underlies much of the analysis by Peter Laut in his evaluation to the development of community pastures in Saskatchewan throughout this century. His paper demonstrates the interplay of environment, personality, and economic circumstances which interacted in the development of policy for management of marginal arable farming land in the dry zone of Saskatchewan. His findings are of considerable interest to historians as well as to those investigating man's adaption to harsh environmental conditions in western Canada.

Two papers deal specifically with the physical environment. The first, by V. Wuorinen, describes the Aiyansh volcano in northern British Columbia and describes why and how the area of that volcano should be preserved for posterity and protected by law from unrestricted use by the general public. The paper by P. Suckling on reflection, heating, and longwave exchange coefficients is a scientific evaluation of the radiation balance of a dwarf apple orchard. Suckling's analysis of heating and longwave exchange coefficients provides results similar to those of other studies, but the author cautions that short-term estimation of net radiation requires further analysis and the application of alternative modelling techniques than those employed in his research.

The final section in this volume contains abstracts of papers presented at the annual meeting of the Western Division but not published in this volume of "Occasional Papers in Geography."

BANQUET SPEECH, LANGARA MEETINGS,
WESTERN DIVISION, C. A. G.,
MARCH 8, 1975

GEOGRAPHY IN THE SEVENTIES

N. V. Scarfe,
The University of British Columbia

In each decade of this century, Geography seems to have under-
gone change in content, in philosophy, and in methods of study. We
have seen a movement from Physiography to Determinism, from an emphasis
on Natural Regions to Economic Geography, from aerial photography to
remote sensing, from regional to systematic Geography, from subjective
interpretation to rigorous quantitative analysis. It would be possible
to recite many other trends but the purpose of this article, however,
is to offer a prediction about the likely developments in the next
ten years by reference to some recent publications.

I shall quote some recent writings which indicate the way in
which Geography of the later 1970's is likely to develop, for it
seems to me that the story of Geography is completing a full circle.
The function, purpose and philosophy of the subject is progressing
away from the morass of the sixties towards the unity, the artistry
and the intellectual rigor of the great thinkers of two generations
ago, but with the added advantages of modern technology, innovative
methods and better teaching. And I hope we are advancing towards a
much better geography which will make more useful contributions to
human welfare and to friendly world-wide collaboration in the use and
conservation of the earth's resources.

A good knowledge of the real world plus the field geographer's
outlook, be it Gilbert White's[1] or Peter Haggett's or David Harvey's
or even my own, ought to be significant in helping to create a more
generous world order.

Something of the flavour and the trends of the 1970's can be
gained from David Harvey's article on "The Role of Theory" published
in 1972. In this interesting article, he talks about theory as the
codification of previous experience or "new dimensions of thinking
about some very old and intriguing geographical problems." He goes
on to say that we haven't been as successful as we had hoped in the

9

past ten years and that "we might have been better advised to have spent more of our time exploring the wealth of ideas and experiences contained in our traditional literature." He says recent work with its rigour and clarity of thinking has simply given us new perspectives on old geographical ideas. He then adds "We can now at very long last return to the Man/Environment relationship." A final quotation from David Harvey says that "Theoretical structure must be closely related to real world observation." The interesting thing is that this is exactly what Isaiah Bowman said when he wrote "Geography in Relation to Social Sciences" in 1934. I was also intrigued by the similarity between what Russell Smith had said years ago in his book on North America and what Harvey said in the last paragraph of his article "The Man/Environment relation as it enters into the learning process is at the very heart of our cultural dynamic."

But it isn't just Harvey who is providing insight into the future. I read with some interest what Dr. C. Glacken wrote in 1967 in his book on "Traces on the Rhodian Shore" because it differed so little from what Carl Sauer[2] had written 50 years ago in 1925, when he said: "In the colourful reality of life there is a continuous resistance of fact to confinement within any simplistic theory. Here are an inexhaustable body of factors and a variety of relations which provide a course of inquiry that does not need to restrict itself to the straits of rationalism."

Coming now to Canada for a moment, I think most of you will know Doctor Relph who works at the University of Toronto. He claims that the world of man is not easily subjected to objective scientific laws of prediction. He goes on to say "The World is thus understood as being essentially subjective and no empirical knowledge, however purged and objectified, can get away from this matrix of all experience." He then adds "The World is understood not as a sum of objects or as a mass of matter but as a system of relations between man and his surroundings."

However, I imagine it was the article of Dr. Leonard Guelke,[3] published in *The Canadian Geographer*, 1971, that really set the stage for a new geography in the seventies for Canada. It seems, too, that he struck a sympathetic chord among the general public, who were being bothered by ecological destruction, pollution and excessive waste of the earth's resources. Surely one of the most urgent challenges now facing mankind is to hold and reverse the growing deterioration of the environment. The biosphere, that thin layer of air, water and soil that surrounds our planet and on which all life on earth depends, is in danger of destruction through abuse and neglect. Pollution may be defined as being artifically induced deterioration of the natural environment of air, water, soil. This may be a health problem, an economic problem, political problem, or an aesthetic problem but it certainly is a geographic problem. We have not yet conquered nature;

we still have to adjust and adapt to it.

In 1974, Dr. E. E. Taaffe[4] wrote "The revival of the man-land or ecological view has reflected society's great surge of interest in environmental questions." Taaffe went on to say: "For the seventies it is hoped that geographic research can maintain a reasonable balance between activism and scientism, by stressing those emerging generalizations which promise to have the greatest impact on society. The spatial view should be more closely articulated to a revitalized man-land view and to the complementary but relatively neglected (Area Study) view."

From the other side of the water I hear this kind of comment: "Why not describe the geographic scene the way it is; in a way which ordinary people can comprehend and recognize: not the ritualized, stylized, bland versions of the text book, but the messy, imprecise, everchanging rough and tumble of human affairs and transactions. We need masterful analyses, not correlation coefficients or differential equations. We do not need the smokescreen of statistics or sub-specialty jargon to dazzle geographers or confuse the laymen. Let's avoid academic gamesmanship and demonstrate the relevance of geography to the solution of current, real-life problems. But let us also avoid trespass on other subjects." So says Barry Floyd[5] from Durham University in 1974.

I think you may all have read Clyde Browning's[6] comments in *The Professional Geographer* in 1974 in which he said that Geography is in real danger of becoming too fragmented in its interests, superficial in its research and spread much too thinly. Two of the criteria which he uses in assessing geography are, "Are the elements of the physical environment, especially those affecting Man, involved?" and "Is the topic useful in a creation of regional synthesis?"

It was, however, my reading of W. W. Bunge[7] on what he calls "The Geography" in *The Professional Geographer* in 1973 that made me choose this particular discourse. In that article and in subsequent comment he ways, "You cannot separate physical and human Geography. Both in theory and in practice, both in the abstract and in the struggle of life, physical and human Geography are one, inseparable, cognate and the same." He said that Geography deals with nature, population and the economy in their unity.

How very similar this is to the words of Vidal de la Blache when, in the early part of this century, he said that the art of Geography is not to divide up what Nature has brought together. Bunge claims that environmentalism should never have been purged. He says it is called for, because mankind is in a survival crisis and Man must learn to live in the context of nature. "How Man interacts with Nature on the earth's surface as the home of Man, is a question that must emerge again in Geography. So we must revive our work on

11

environmentalism. Physical Geography needs a new prominence even in the urban city."

Environmental conditions of the place where people live matters to those who live there. Furthermore, studies of these conditions always involve a primary consideration of the air, water and land at that place. If pollution means anything, it means destruction of the physical conditions necessary for human existence. Just those land, water, and air conditions are the essential core of geography and it seems to me that we are now reassessing our Geography to bring the diversity of the sixties into a unity such as was conceived by Jean Bruhnes and Sir Halford MacKinder many years back.

The integration of knowledge can just as easily happen around the focus of Geography as it can around any other focus. Earth Science and Social Science should be related very closely by means of Geography. Instead we have many pseudo-social scientists called "geographers" integrating their ideas around Sociology and earth scientists integrating their's around Biology and so splitting Geography apart into two non-functional areas.

Geography is an integrated way of looking at the world because it is then very useful in helping others see the sense of man using the earth's resources wisely in an atmosphere of international goodwill. So I tend to look on the sixties as a time when we were fashioning instruments and methods for making the older Geography more efficient and more useful to the world.

As Browning says, we should concern ourselves much more with the central concepts of Geography not so much with its boundaries. And finally, may I take a quote from a book written in 1914: it says "Nature has been so silent in her persistent influence over Man, that the geographic factor in the equation of human development has been overlooked." We would of course now substitute the word "environmental" for "geographic." However, it is just as true now. And, of course, you know who wrote it--Ellen Churchill Semple!!

In the most recent issue of *The Journal of Geography* (January, 1975), I noticed that the first three out of four full page advertisements are for books on "Physical Geography," but with subtitled "Environment and Man" and "The Environment of Mankind."

In the 1970's, it seems that good Geography is coming back into its own. We are again looking at the real landscape but more closely and critically than before. We are basing our theory first on real outdoor study and arriving at models and games at the end after getting our feet wet. And the physical and human aspects of the world are being closely related. Man and land are seen to be closely interdependent. And that means that good Geography is necessary for understanding modern life and thought.

ABBREVIATED REFERENCES

[1] See *The Professional Geographer*, May 1972, 101-104.

[2] J. Leighly, *A Selection from the Writings of Carl Sauer*, 1967.

[3] *The Canadian Geographer*, Spring, 1971, 38-53.

[4] *Annals of the Association of American Geographers*, March, 1974, 1-16.

[5] *The Professional Geographer*, August, 1974, 320-321.

[6] *The Professional Geographer*, May, 1974, 137-139.

[7] *The Professional Geographer*, Nov., 1973, 331-337, and Feb. 1974, 104-105.

GEOGRAPHERS AND ENERGY

J.D. Chapman
The University of British Columbia

One of today's overriding social issues is popularly referred
to as "the energy crisis" and one of the paradigms emerging in a
variety of disciplines in the academic world is labelled "energetics"
--the energy inputs, transformations and outputs of identified systems.

It is the purpose of this paper briefly to review the diffusion of "energetics" into geography generally, and then within this
to sketch the progress of the study of energy in the more restricted
terms of economic geography.

THE DIFFUSION OF "ENERGETICS" INTO GEOGRAPHY

Early in 1965 D. Linton delivered a Presidential Address to
the British Geographical Association entitled, "The Geography of
Energy,"[1] using precisely the same title as that of two books, one
written by P. George in 1950[2] and the other by G. Manners in 1964.[3]
Linton emphasized at the outset of his paper that these and other
similar works[4]:

> . . . deal only with a small part of the field that is my
> present concern . . . [namely] . . . the economic geography
> of mechanical and electrical energy. . . . [This] is certainly
> not my subject. That subject is literally the geography of
> energy with no qualifications as to either the kind of geo-
> graphy or the kind of energy.[5]

and later, that:

> . . . we have to consider energy inputs from all sources and
> the geography of any area under study is the product of the
> interacting operation of both natural and vital energy.[6]

Let us speculate on the extent to which these views have
been heeded and examine the routes by which a stress upon what

15

Linton calls natural and vital energy have entered geography commencing with some of those subfields particularly concerned with the physical environment.

As the static, classificatory style of climatology became increasingly influenced by meteorology it turned toward process oriented, dynamic studies. One of the earliest and still today one of the most ardent advocates of energy based studies is F. K. Hare who, as early as 1953, published a little book entitled *The Restless Atmosphere*:

> . . . was written to fill a gap in the literature of physical geography . . . in the no-man's land of dynamic climatology . . . [7]

and in which the first chapter was devoted to "The Energy of the Atmosphere." During the 1950's the "energy exchange" focus in climatology received a considerable fillip from the work of M. I. Budyko in the U.S.S.R.[8] and C. W. Thornthwaite in the U.S.A. Thornthwaite in his Presidential Address to the Association of American Geographers in 1961 stressed the importance to climatology of an understanding of the:

> . . . nature of the exchange of momentum, heat and moisture between the earth's surface and the atmosphere . . . [9]

and later went so far as to recommend that:

> . . . in some centre of learning in this country we should undertake to reshape geographical theory on the basis of heat and moisture exchange.[10]

Judging from a rather superficial sampling of climatology literature it appears as though, during the last two decades, the conversion of climatology to a dynamic, energy-moisture based study has become almost complete.

In geomorphology a similar sequence has unfolded as the physics and applied-science based work of Strahler, Leopold and Langbein and others led to the emergence of dynamic geomorphology. The introduction and interpretation of this "new" geomorphology to geography was, to a considerable extent, set in the context of General Systems theory and systems analysis derived from the biological sciences. By 1969 the author of a small book in the *Foundations of Earth Science Series* writes that:

> A major goal of geomorphology is to understand how the immense energy of solar radiation is converted into mechanical work that shapes landscapes.[11]

Starting with the work of Lindeman[12] in the early forties, the study of the flow of energy in and out of biological environments has developed into a major concern for "energetics" in biological ecology. Although Russian biogeographers appear to do a good deal of work of this kind, other geographers (as distinct from biologists) in their contribution to the biogeographical literature[13] appear to have neglected "energetics" until quite recently.

Beyond being identified as an underlying organizing basis for studies in the individual subfields of physical geography, a focus on "energetics" has recently been advocated as providing a unifying theme for physical geography and, even more generally, for environment-man studies.

Russian geographers have sought and found a considerable degree of unity in their physical geography studies through their emphasis upon energy balance studies. However, it is only in the last five years that there have been noteworthy attempts to use "energetics" as the major, or at least a major, unifying framework for Physical Geography in North America. For example, D. H. Miller's survey course in physical geography entitled "The Energy and Mass Budget at the Surface of the Earth" proposes to deal with the earth's surface:

. . . in terms of the streams of energy and matter that come to it and leave it, are transformed at it and themselves influence natural and cultural phenomena at and near it.[14]

Similarly D. Carter and associates in another course outline while stressing the value of focussing upon the "interface" as a unifying theme for physical geography rely heavily upon:

. . . the schemes of allocation for energy and materials which determine relative amounts and timing of work in the interface environmental systems.[15]

Professor Hare has not only continued to advocate and demonstrate the beneifts of energy exchange studies in climatology over the last fifteen years but most recently has argued for their ability to afford a unifying force among the sub-disciplines involved in physical and biological enquiry. In a paper that pays strong tribute to Budyko and Gerasimov, he writes:

. . . I am hopeful that the crystallization of climatology around energy considerations will help to lead toward the deserved synthesis [of the sub-disciplines that study the earth's surface].[16]

Yet another example is Chorley and Kennedy's book *Physical Geography: A Systems Approach*. As the title suggests it is through systems theory that the authors claim a new identity will emerge for physical geography but within this they place considerable emphasis upon:

> . . . the manner in which the throughput of energy tends to produce and maintain a discernible organization, characterized by hierarchical differentiation.[17]

Implied in several of these cited works is the role that the study of "energetics" may play as a unifying force at a still higher level of generalization--namely the study of environment and man.   In the recent Resource Paper, "Man and Environment: Conceptual Frameworks," Hare extends his views to this broader context:

> We have stressed the energy relations of ecosystems because of their obvious link with other concerns of the geographer-- with physical climatology, with food supply and with human energy requirements.[18]

Strahler's well-known *Physical Geography* has now become in one of its forms, *An Introduction to Environmental Science* throughout which what is called the "energy system" is used as a fundamental concept:

> . . . for it provides the one framework common to all branches of environmental science, from the study of the earth's atmosphere to the study of its ecology.   Man . . . [also] is a significant part of the earth's energy system.[19]

Finally in this context mention may be made of Simmons' book, *The Ecology of Natural Resources*, in which he writes that:

> . . . in all ecosystems, as indeed in all studies of resource processes the role of energy is crucial.[20]

Let us now look briefly at the role of the social sciences and humanities in introducing "energetics" into geography.   It has been notably less than that from the bio-physical and applied sciences but present all the same.   The geographer-economist E. W. Zimmerman[21] presented the role of energy in society in a powerful and durable manner in his classic, *World Resources and Industries*, first published in 1933.   Surprisingly, however, this potentially valuable framework was not developed in any sustained way by geographers although there were individual exceptions as far apart as H. V. Warren at The University of British Columbia and N. Kolosovskiy in Moscow.   The latter,[22] in the context of a national discussion on the separate existence of physical and economic geography, wrote, in 1950, to a colleague in Leningrad as follows:

> After Marx all social sciences use Marxist measures--the mean socially needed amount of working time--man-hours.

Scientific technology, please note, uses a derivative unit of account, i.e., the ratio:

$$\frac{\text{physical measurement units}}{\text{amount of working time}} \quad \text{for example} \quad \frac{\text{kilowatt-hours}}{\text{man-hours}}$$

Today among geographers only Dan Luten of Berkeley seems to be writing in this vein. In the "Energy & Power" issue of *Scientific American* (1971), he wrote:

> Only those men who can convert heat and other forms of energy to work and can apply that work where they will, can travel over the world and shape it to their ends. The crux of the matter is the generation of work--the conversion of energy and its delivery to the point of application.[23]

Even the study of the economic geography of energy has attracted relatively few geographers. After a promising start with F. Hjulstrom's[24] monograph on electricity in 1942 and Pierre George's[25] book *Geographie de l'energie* in 1950, little significant work appeared until the early sixties when books by Chardonnet, Manners and O'Dell[26] suggested that the ground work was done and that the energy industry was to become one of the regularly recognized topics of economic geographical enquiry. However, little development took place. The journals contain a scattering of papers on aspects of oil, electricity and coal; one or two economic geography texts recognize the existence of an energy industry and attempt to set energy in its broader context.[27]

In the last three or four years there are once again promising signs. Several energy-oriented economic geographers have emerged or re-emerged such as P. O'Dell, Director of the Geographic Institute of the Netherlands School of Economics at Rotterdam who has become a prolific writer and active participant at high levels of the energy scene in Western Europe.[28] In addition to O'Dell's work, titles on energy have recently appeared in the several so-called "Foundation" series of various publishers as well as in some University geography department series. The most notable of these in the present context is N. B. Guyol's[29] little book, *Energy in the Perspective of Geography*, in which he sees a principal objective of what he calls the "science of energy" to be the explanation of the spatial and temporal variations in energy requirements. He deals effectively with energy accounting in commodity and sector terms and reviews factors influencing energy demand by sector. This latter is in itself a refreshing and needed departure from the usual preoccupation with production and transport. Equally refreshing and welcome is the treatment in two recently published paperbacks[30] of commercial energy in the context of environmental impact, the article by D. Luten[31] already referred to in the *Scientific American* issue on Energy and Power, and in the first issue of *Energy Policy*, two

19

articles by the geographers, Peter O'Dell and Leslie Dienes[32]--in
their different ways these two articles are both concerned with
basically the same questions: what are the spatial linkages involved in supplying fuel to the respective areas with which they are
dealing (West Europe and U.S.S.R.), what factors influence choices
among the actual and potential linkages, and what policy options are
available.

In summary, it may be said that "energetics" has diffused
widely, though differentially, into the realm of physical geography
but its effectiveness as a unifying theme is still probably more
advocated than demonstrated, that an approach has been made to using
"energetics" as an organizing framework for the study of interactions
between environment and man--an approach which is coming more from
oriented quarters toward physical science than toward social science,
and, lastly, that the economic geography of energy is receiving sustained and sophisticated study by less than half-a-dozen geographers!

THE ECONOMIC GEOGRAPHY OF ENERGY

Before turning to the second and shorter part of this paper
which is concerned with the future of "energetics" in the context of
economic geography, one or two assumptions which lie behind the
opinions to be expressed should be made explicit. First, it is
assumed that geographers have something to say about the commercial
energy scene and, when and if we enter this arena, we should do so
on our own terms. That is to say, let us ask the questions which
our disciplinary background prepares us to answer rather than questions better answered by others. It is the writer's opinion that
this involves asking questions about spatial organization and environmental interaction.

Secondly, it is envisaged that the development of a field of
enquiry may go forward at several levels at once.[33] There is *research*,
a term which is best reserved for the quest for really new and pene-
trating knowledge and insights (what has been called frontier research); there is *study* or *disciplined enquiry* which usually results
in a widening rather than advancing of knowledge; and there is *teaching*, the presentation of the results of work at the other two levels
in a manner which stimulates interest, encourages curiosity and com-
pletes the cycle by nourishing disciplined study and research.

In this general context what might geographers be doing in
the research sense? The two suggestions which follow should be pre-
faced by mention of some of the studies and programmes which have
recently become available on research requirements from a more general point of view. For example there is *Energy and the Social
Sciences: An Examination of Research Needs*,[34] the last of three
studies conducted in almost as many years by Resources for the Future
in Washington; organizations such as the Electric Power Institute of

Palo Alto, the MIT Energy Laboratory, the Energy Research Groups at
the Open University and University of London, and others have all
more or less well-formulated research programmes. From these
sources one can see what is underway and assess those areas in which
geographers might profitably work.

The first of the two suggestions that I have comes from the
RFF work just mentioned in which the authors state:

> A particularly interesting, although exceedingly complex con-
> cept, would be a model of the energy/environmental system
> which through the inclusion of underlying natural processes
> could show the ecological alterations that stem from energy
> production and consumption and then the feed back effects
> that the changes in the natural system will have on man him-
> self.[35]

Such a topic would be complex indeed but could well become the focus
of a team of geographers with both physical and social scientific
interests.

Secondly, and still in the research category, is a group of
studies clustered around the analysis of the spatial dimensions of
large scale commercial energy systems. Numerous attempts are now
underway at modelling commercial energy systems at scales ranging
from world to national, sub-national and company space.[36] Few have
explicit spatial components within them and even in those that do,
few if any geographers are involved. The development of appropriate methodologies, techniques and terminology in an abstract way
would in itself be an innovative contribution to the rapidly emerging field of modelling "commercial energetics."

Turning to the second category of enquiry, referred to as
energy "studies" rather than energy "research," there is a much
greater range to choose from. However, mention is made here of
only one--the economic geography of energy consumption. There is
not space to develop this at any length but perhaps it would be
useful to sketch some of the elements of a study of energy consumption at the urban/metropolitan scale. In the first place, the
choice of this scale is significant in itself because although the
bulk of energy consumption is carried on in urban/metropolitan
centres, where are the studies at this scale? One is underway of
the New York area, another is nearly completed on Hong Kong by a
Ph.D. student at the Australian National University, and a study of
Sydney has already been written up by workers at CSIRO in Canberra.[37]

Initially some descriptive studies of several centres are
required to determine the spatial distribution of energy consumption
within the city to be followed by more analytical work on particular
sectors. For example the Commercial Sector, which consumes some

15-16% of all energy in Canada, is probably 100% concentrated in cities and yet one is hardly able to specify what is included in the category let alone say anything about the consumption mix, conversion efficiencies, etc. The main difficulty with urban based energy studies will be access to data although much of it is already in the hands of the public utilities.

CONCLUSION

The diffusion of the broad concepts of "energetics" into geography has been going on for at least the last two decades. The long-developed focus of physical and applied scientists upon energy and matter inevitably spread into fields which impinged upon geography. Thus the physicist's interest in energy naturally formed an integral part of the study of the physics of the atmosphere or meteorology which in turn spread to physical climatology and later to climatology *per se*; the biologist's development of concepts of trophic levels and "energetic ecology" are just now impinging upon the geographic consciousness while, earlier, the introduction of energy and mass balance concepts necessarily accompanied the emergence of dynamic geomorphology. Similarly, though less obviously, it appears as if economic interest in "work" in the sense of human labour and productivity led E.W. Zimmerman in the thirties to incorporate energy so fundamentally in his writings.

The more recent claims for "energetics" as a unifying force between the several sub-disciplines of physical geography have been further extended to include the study of the interactions between environment and man. It appears that there is considerable potential in this latter extension for both fruitful research and innovative teaching in a manner which will foster cohesion between physical and human geographers. The concepts of energetics in conjunction with systems analysis as an enabling methodology seem to afford a combination which can contribute significantly to attaining a synethesis of many of the otherwise all too disparate interests of geographers.[38]

REFERENCES

[1] D. Linton, "The Geography of Energy," *Geography*, L, (1965), 197-228.

[2] P. George, *Geographie de L'Energie* (Paris: Libraire de Medicis, 1950).

[3] G. Manners, *The Geography of Energy* (London: Hutchinson University Library, 1964).

[4] See for instance: J. Chardonnet, *Les Sources d'Energie* (Paris: Editions Sirey, 1962), and J.D. Chapman, "A Geography of Energy," *Canadian Geographer*, 5, (1961), 10-15.

[5] Linton, *op. cit.*, 197.

[6] Linton, *op. cit.*, 198.

[7] F.K. Hare, *The Restless Atmosphere* (London: Hutchinson University Library, 1953), VII.

[8] M.I. Budyko, *The Heat Balance of the Earth's Surface*, (Leningrad: 1956), (Translated by N.A. Stepanova, U.S. Weather Bureau, Washington, D.C., 1958).

[9] C.W. Thornwaite, "The Task Ahead," *Annals. Assoc. of American Geographers*, 51, (1961), 349.

[10] Thornthwaite, *op. cit.*, 354.

[11] A.L. Bloom, *The Surface of the Earth* (New Jersey: Prentice Hall, 1969), 8.

[12] R.L. Lindeman, "The trophic-dynamic aspect of ecology," *Ecology*, 23, (1942), 399-418.

[13] A sampling of *Geographical Abstracts, Series B--Biogeography Section* from 1965-1974 supports this impression. However, the first issue of the *Journal of Biogeography* suggests a change.

[14] D.H. Miller, *A Survey Course: The Energy and Mass Budget at the Surface of the Earth* (Washington, D.C.: AAG Commission on College Geography #7, 1968), 1.

[15] D.B. Carter, *et al.*, *The Interface as a Working Environment: A Purpose for Physical Geography* (Washington, D.C.: AAG Commission on College Geography, Technical Paper #7, 1972), 10.

[16] F.K. Hare, "Energy Based Climatology and Its Frontier with Ecology," Chapter 8 in R.J. Chorley (ed.) *Directions in Geography* (London: Methuen, 1973), 172.

[17] R.J. Chorley and B.A. Kennedy, *Physical Geography: A Systems Approach* (London: Prentice Hall Int., 1971), 3.

[18] K. Hewitt and F.K. Hare, *Man and Environment: Conceptual Frameworks* (Washington, D.C.: AAG Commission on College Geography, Resource Paper #20, 1973), 27.

[19] A.N. Strahler and A.H. Strahler, *Introduction to Environmental Science* (Santa Barbara: Hamilton, 1974), 9.

[20] I.G. Simmons, *The Ecology of Natural Resources* (London: Arnold, 1974), 6.

[21] E.W. Zimmerman, *World Resources and Industries* (New York: Harper, 1933).

[22] N.N. Kolosovskiy, "On the Concept of the Unity of Geography," *Soviet Geography*, III (1962), 42.

[23] D.B. Luten, "The Economic Geography of Energy," *Scientific American*, 224, (1971), 165.

[24] F. Hjulstrom, *The Economic Geography of Electricity: An Outline* (Uppsala: Geographical Institute #12, 1942).

[25] George, *op. cit.*

[26] Chardonnet, *op. cit.*; P. O'Dell, *An Economic Geography of Oil* (London: Bell, 1963); Manners, *op. cit.*

[27] For example: R.S. Thoman, *et al.*, *The Geography of Economic Activity* (New York: McGraw Hill, 1968).

[28] P. O'Dell, *Natural Gas in W. Europe: A Case Study in the Economic Geography of Energy Resources* (Haarlem: Bohn, 1969); "Europe's Oil," *Geographical Journal*, 13, (1973); *Oil and World Power* (London: Penguin, 1974); *Energy Needs and Resources* (Toronto: MacMillan, 1974).

[29] N.B. Guyol, *Energy in the Perspective of Geography* (New Jersey: Prentice Hall, 1971).

[30] W.M. Ross, *Oil Pollution as an International Problem* (Victoria, B.C.: W. Geographical Serices #6, 1973); V. Smil, *Energy and the Environment: A long range forecasting study* (Winnipeg: Manitoba Geographical Series #3, 1974).

[31] Luten, *op. cit.*

[32] L. Dienes, "Geographical Problems of Allocation in the Soviet Fuel Supply," *Energy Policy*, I, (1973), 3-20; P. O'Dell, "Indigenous Oil and Gas Developments and W. Europe's Energy Policy Options," *Energy Policy*, I, (1973), 47-64.

[33] H.H. Landsberg, *et al.*, *Energy and the Social Sciences: An Examination of Research Needs* (Washington, D.C.: Resources for the Future, 1974), 6.

[34] Landsberg, *op. cit.*

[35] Landsberg, *op. cit.*, 100.

[36] See for example: I.P.C., Science and Technology Press, *Energy Modelling* (Guildford: 1974); International Institute for Applied Systems Analysis, *Proceedings of IIASA Working Seminar on Energy Modelling* (Schloss Luxemburg: 1974).

[37] See for example: M.F. Fels and M.J. Munson, *Energy Thrift in Urban Transportation: Options for the Future* (Peinceton, Center for Environmental Studies #10, 1974); Regional Plan Association and Resources for the Future, *Regional Energy Consumption* (New York: 1974); J.D. Kalma, *et al.*, "Energy Use in the Sydney Area," *The City as a Life System*, Proceedings of the Ecological Society of Australia, 7, (1973), 125-142.

[38] I am particularly indebted to M.C. Church and O. Slaymaker for their critical comments on earlier drafts of this short paper.

PROBLEMS IN THE APPLICATION OF GRAPH-THEORETIC
MEASURES TO TRANSPORTATION NETWORK GROWTH--
A CASE STUDY OF ALBERTA HIGHWAYS

P.C. Monanu and M.J. Hodgson
University of Alberta

The structural complexity of a region's transportation system is considered to be a correlate or indicator of the complexity or level of development of the region's economic and settlement system.[1] In recent years, geographers have turned to the use of graph-theoretic measures to evaluate and describe the topological complexities of networks. Garrison and Marble[2] and Kansky[3] have statistically related such measures to levels of national and regional development. Taaffe and Gauthier[4] discuss the application of the measures to the developing complexity of a particular transportation network over time. This paper investigates and attempts to solve some problems arising from attempts to employ these measures in this latter context. Empirically, the paper focusses upon the growth of the highway and urban systems of the province of Alberta, 1934-1974.

The structural characteristics of the highway network are considered at five points in time, 1934, 1948,[5] 1954, 1964, and 1974. In order to provide a system of interest for 1934 and one of manageable proportions for 1974, a centre is considered to be a node or vertex if its population exceeds 2000.[6] Centres which form part of metropolitan areas are considered to be systematically related to these centres and are not treated separately. Links or edges are defined as highway connections between centres, whether paved or not. Figures 1 and 2 illustrate the networks of 1934 and 1974, and Figure 3 the graph abstractions upon which the analysis is based. Problems arising within the network-modelling procedures are discussed in Hodgson and Smith[7] and Jackson.[8] In all cases, the networks are considered to be planar--in that the intersection of two links is considered to create a new node within the system.

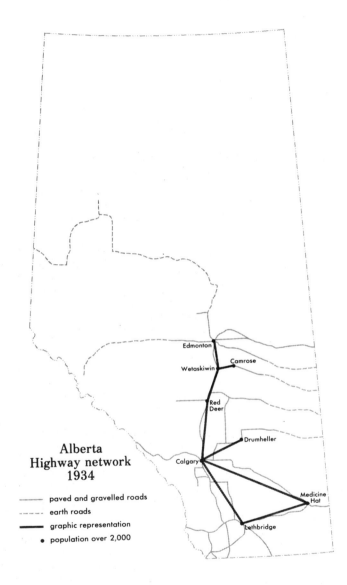

Alberta
Highway network
1934

——— paved and gravelled roads

- - - - earth roads

——— graphic representation

• population over 2,000

Edmonton

Camrose

Wetaskiwin

Red
Deer

Drumheller

Calgary

Medicine
Hat

Lethbridge

Figure 1.

26

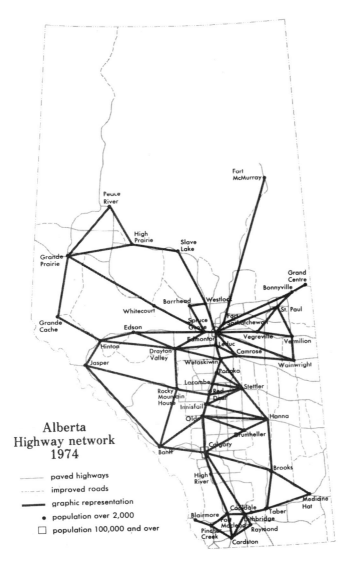

Figure 2.

Graph-theoretic indices for
the highway system of Alberta, 1934-1974

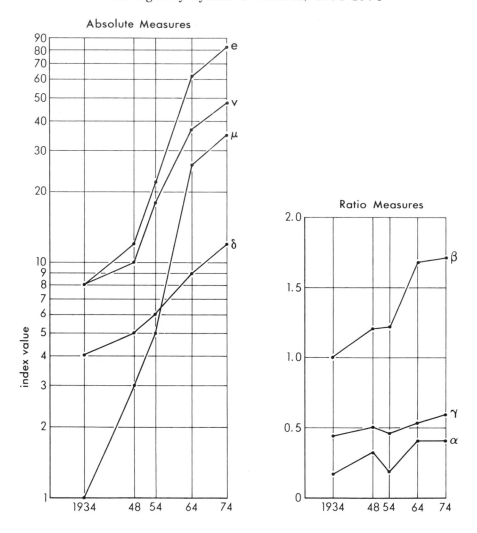

Figure 3.

GRAPH-THEORETIC INDICES OF NETWORK TOPOLOGY

Many indices of network structure have appeared in the geographical literature.[9] These may be characterized as being network-specific, describing some aspect of overall network complexity, or node-specific, describing the relative position of a particular centre within a network's structure. Among the more commonly employed measures are ones depending solely upon considerations of topology or connectiveness, and ones which also take link lengths and their circuitousness into account. This study considers several topological network-specific indices which depend solely upon values of three parameters, the number of links, or *edges* (e), the number of nodes or *vertices* (v), and the number of isolated subgraphs (discrete subnetworks). Table I presents the values of these indices which are now briefly described.

TABLE I

Graph-theoretic Indices for the Alberta
Highway Network, 1934-1974

Measure	1934	1948	1954	1964	1974
Number of Nodes (v)	8	10	18	37	48
Number of lines (e)	8	12	22	62	82
Number of Isolated subgraphs (p)	1	1	1	1	1
β	1.00	1.20	1.22	1.68	1.71
γ	.44	.50	.46	.53	59
μ	1	3	5	26	35
α	.17	.33	.19	.41	.41
δ	5	5	6	9	12

Source: Official Alberta Roadmaps

The first two measures deal with the relationship between the numbers of edges and vertices within a graph. The conceptual basis for these indices is the notion that a larger number of links within a settlement system is indicative of greater network complexity. The *beta* index,

$$\beta = \frac{e}{v}$$

is a simple ratio of edges to vertices. In planar graphs, β ranges from 0 to 3.0, and would be expected to increase over time as a network increases in complexity. A more meaningful form of the relationship between edge and vertex numbers is provided by the *gamma* index,

$$\gamma = \frac{e}{3 \ (v-2)}$$

This is, in fact, the ratio of the observed number of edges to the

29

maximum possible number within a system of v vertices. Its value
ranges from 0 to a maximum of 1.0 in a fully-connected system, and
would be expected to increase with a network's increasing complexity.

These measures only deal implicitly with the actual structural complexity of a network. The following two indices consider
the number of circuits within a system, the importance of which a-
rises from the provision of alternative routings, and in many cases,
the shortening of paths between centres. The *cyclomatic number*,

$$\mu = e-v+p$$

directly indicates the number of fundamental circuits in a graph.
The 1934 value of 1 arises from the Calgary-Lethbridge-Medicine Hat
circuit. The relationship between a particular network's circuity
and complexity is the *alpha* index,

$$\alpha = \frac{\mu}{2v - 5}$$

relating the observed number of fundamental circuits to the maximum
number. Increasing network complexity should be accompanied by increasing values of μ and α.

A network's *diameter*, δ, is defined as the longest internodal
shortest path in the network; the 1934 value of 4 indicates the minimum number of links which must be traversed in order to travel between Edmonton and Lethbridge or Medicine Hat. Unlike any of the
above indices, the diameter is an indicator of a network's topological extent.

URBAN AND HIGHWAY SYSTEM EXPANSION IN ALBERTA, 1931-1934

Alberta's population increased by 122 per cent over the
study period, with absolute increase more than attributable to urban
growth (Table II). The number of urban centres (Table   increased six-fold, and the "percentage of population urban" column
documents the transition from an agrarian rural province to a
reasonably urbanized one. Highway mileage (Table 11-B) increased
by more than 300 per cent, a figure undoubtedly biased by the exclusion of earth roads, presumably more important in the earlier
years. The concomitant growth of population centres and highway
mileage (Table II-C) is to be expected in a developing system, but
it is instructive to consider the elements of this relationship more
closely. Per capita highway mileage, which has been related to
economic development in developing areas,[10] increased over the
early stages. The drop in these figures in the last period suggests
a level of relative highway saturation, allowing population growth
to outstrip the increase in mileage. This feature is more strik-
ingly evident in the "miles per urban place"[11] and "miles per 1000
urban persons" figures. When the length of the urban system's useful connections (graph-link miles) is considered, per capita mileage

TABLE II

Urban and Highway System Characteristics

A: Urban Population Growth[1]

Year	Rural	Population Urban	Total	% of Popula- Urban	Number of Urban Places
1931	453,097	196,461	731,605	26.9	8
1946	489,583	261,544	796,169	32.9	10
1951	489,826	393,365	939,501	41.9	18
1961	488,733	768,838	1,331,944	57.7	37
1971	431,620	1,161,025	1,627,875	71.3	48

Source: *Census of Canada*

B: Highway Mileage Growth[2]

Year	Surfaced	Gravel	Total	Graph Lines[3]
1934	80	2,261	2,341	724
1948	735	9,469	10,204	1,039
1954	2,119	28,154	30,273	2,094
1964	4,989	54,541	59,530	4,798
1971	5,796	64,903	70,699	6,135

Source: *Canada Year Book*

C: Relation of Highway Mileage to Population

Years	Miles Per 1000 Persons	Miles per 1000 Urban Persons	Graph-line[3] Miles Per 1000 Urban Persons	Miles Per Urban Place
1934/31	3.2	11.9	3.7	292.6
1948/46	12.8	39.0	3.8	1020.4
1954/51	32.2	77.0	5.3	1681.8
1964/61	44.7	77.4	6.2	1608.9
1974/71	43.4	60.9	5.3	1473.9

[1] For the purposes of this study, network nodes (centres of over 2,000 population) are considered to be urban.

[2] Figures are totals for the province. Earth roads are not taken into account due to the fact that figures contain road allowances in some years and exclude them in others.

[3] These figures portray the actual highway mileage which would be traversed in travelling the modelled links.

31

increases at a much lower rate, suggesting that a large proportion
of the province's highway growth has been directed toward serving
the agricultural hinterland rather than toward the improvement of
urban interconnection. The raw population and mileage figures document the growth, in absolute terms, of the province's urban and
highway infrastructure. They contribute nothing, however, to an
understanding of the topological complexity of these systems.

GRAPH-THEORETIC INDICES FOR THE HIGHWAY
SYSTEM OF ALBERTA, 1934-1974

Comparison of Figures 1 and 2 illustrates the considerable
increase in spatial extent and apparent complexity of the network
of urban places and their interconnections, the parsimonious system
of 1934 having evolved into a maze of nodes, linkages, and circuits
by 1974. The graph-theoretic measures (Table I, Figure 3) are
meant to be objective indices of the structural complexity of the
highway network, but they contain certain inconsistencies. The
values, v, e, and μ, plotted on a logarithmic scale to facilitate
the observation of *rate* of change, document the increased numbers
of nodes, links, and circuits apparent in the maps. The network
diameter also shows a steady rate of increase over the period.
Although these measures provide evidence of the increased complexity of the entire system, they say nothing of the complexity or
adequacy of the highway network with respect to the service of the
expanded urban system.

As the number of centres within an urban system increases,
the number of linkages required to connect them, and the number of
circuits required to provide movement efficiency, must also increase.
The three ratio measures, β, γ, and α allow the consideration of
network complexity in this context. The value of β, the simple
ratio of edges to vertices, increases throughout the period, although
its very slight increase between 1948 and 1954 is evidence that the
urban system nearly outstripped that of the highways. As the number
of nodes in a system grows, the potential number of links among them
grows at roughly three times their rate. The gamma index shows that
in the 1948-1954 period, the number of edges fell behind previous
trends in this respect, and that over the entire period, the number
of edges has made relatively slight advances toward achieving its
potential. As the number of nodes within a system rises, the potential number of fundamental circuits rises as roughly twice their
number; α indicates the degree to which the network has achieved its
potential in this respect. In these terms, the Alberta network de-
clined in complexity in the 1948-1954 period and remained stationary
between 1964 and 1974. Thus, as the overall system expands over the
study period, some indicators of network structure increase while
others fluctuate. Assuming that most transportation networks of
interest function within non-stagnant urban systems, there appear

32

to be substantial difficulties in employing standard network evaluation measures meaningfully in a time-series context.

GRAPH-THEORETIC NETWORK INDICES IN A "CONSTANT" ALBERTA URBAN SYSTEM

Taaffe and Gauthier[12] suggest the utility of graph-theoretic
indices in the study of network evolution within a fixed city system.
This section investigates such an approach to assessing the growth
of the Alberta highway network. The final (1974) state is assumed
to represent a climax city system toward which the Alberta situation
evolved over the study period. Table III presents values of the
ratio indices over time, when 48 vertices are used in each period.
The indices calculated in this way provide a certain satisfaction by
virtue of the way they increase in what intuitively appears to be an
increasingly complex system, and by their consistency with the non-
ratio measures. Their increase is, of course, guaranteed because
they are ratios of the number of edges or circuits to a function of
the constant v.

TABLE III

Graph-theoretic Indices in a 48-node
Alberta System, 1934-1974

Measure	1934	1948	1954	1964	1974
β	.16	.25	.46	1.29	1.71
γ	.06	.09	.16	.45	.59
α*	.01	.03	.06	.30	.41

$$* \quad \alpha \text{ is defined here as: } \frac{\text{number of fundamental circuits}}{2V - 5}$$

This approach is open to criticism on several counts. The
assumption that the most recent urban system represents the final
stage of some evolutionary process is clearly unrealistic, but is
essential if the γ and α ratios are to have any meaning. The consideration of some places as nodes at times when they may not have
existed is also somewhat distasteful. It is also possible that
important ways in which networks *do* decrease in complexity or
adequacy over particular periods are ignored when a deliberate
effort is made to force consistancy upon the indices used. It is
difficult to address such problems without a deeper understanding
of the meaning of the various indices.

33

DISCUSSION

This paper has applied several standard network evaluation measures to the growing highway network of Alberta. In addition to providing a certain amount of empirical information, it is hoped that some question of the utility and meaning of these measures has been raised. Measures of absolute link and circuit numbers provide numerical values for visual impressions gained from the maps. Difficulties arise from the use of more complex ratio measures relating the number of such features to their potential numbers. Dealing in values which are not visually apparent, these indices are more difficult to interpret.

The provision of interurban transportation networks may be viewed as a trade-off between the costs of travel within the system and the costs of network construction and maintenance. As the number of linkages serving a set of urban centres increases, travel costs are reduced, but by decreasing amounts.[13] The provision of initial interconnection results in considerable travel cost savings, while linkages such as the addition of a direct Edmonton-Red Deer connection to the 1934 network (also providing another circuit) would reduce travel costs marginally at a high capital cost. Obviously, at certain levels of development, the cost of provision of additional "potential" linkages and circuits would outweigh the benefits derived. Rational development policies would surely apply scarce capital resources to other uses when such levels are reached. Thus, the intelligent economic development of any area would not be tied to the achievement of γ and α levels past certain thresholds, much lower than 1.00, these being determined in particular cases by the economic and spatial structures of the urban system.

The main difficulty with this study arises from the use of simple structural assessors in dealing with extremely complex systems. On the other hand, the use of these measures can provide some insight into the growth and adequacy of transportation networks. It is hoped that this paper has suggested the utility of graph-theoretic measures, as well as the danger of imputing too much importance to them as indicators of economic development. Clearly, considerable investigation is required before it is possible to evaluate properly transport network structures in evolving economic systems. It is suggested that such effort is warranted.

SOURCES

[1] See for instance, F.J. Taafe, R.L. Morrill, and P.R. Gould, "Transport expansion in under-developed countries: a comparative analysis," *Geographical Review*, 53, (1963), 503-529.

[2] W.L. Garrison and D.F. Marble, *A Prologomenon to the Forecasting of Transportation Development*, Northwestern University Press, (1965).

[3] K.J. Kansky, *Structure of Transport Networks: Relationships between Network Geometry and Regional Characteristics*, Chicago University Press, (1963).

[4] E.J. Taaffe and H. Gauthier, *Geography of Transportation*, (Englewood Cliffs: Prentice Hall, 1973).

[5] No highway map was available for 1944.

[6] The sources are the *Census of Canada* and the *Canada Year Book*.

[7] M.J. Hodgson and B.G. Smith, "Structural Characteristics of the Highway Networks of Canada's Three Western-most Provinces," *Lethbridge Papers*, B.C. Occasional Series in Geography (1975).

[8] Jackson, "Some Operational and Conceptual Problems of Graph Theory," Geographical Articles, No. 14, Dept. of Geography, Cambridge University, (1973), 10-24.

[9] Most of these are described by Kansky, *op. cit.* Others appear in W.L. Garrison, "Connectivity of the Interstate Highway System," *Regional Science Association, Paper and Proceedings*, 6, (1960), 121-137; and F.R. Pitts, "A Graph-theoretic Approach to Historical Geography," *Professional Geographer*, 17, (1965), 15-20.

[10] Taaffe, *et al., op. cit.*

[11] This is one form of Kansky's *theta* (θ) index.

[12] Taaffe and Gauthier, *op. cit.*

[13] This statement presumes a rational strategy of network construction.

INTER-INDUSTRY MANUFACTURING LINKAGES
WITHIN ALBERTA

Brenton M. Barr, The University of Calgary
Kenneth J. Fairbairn, The University of Alberta

INTRODUCTION

The Problem

The industrial prowess or magnitude of production of urban manufacturing systems is usually inferred from criteria such as numbers employed, the number of industrial establishments, value added through manufacturing, and selling value of factory shipments. Data to measure and assess these criteria are reasonably accessible for most urban areas in Canada and are collected and published by federal and provincial governments. The functional importance of Canadian urban manufacturing places, however, cannot be measured directly from published data since these data are neither collected universally by government nor published in any consistent manner by other agencies. The general economic relation of any urban manufacturing economy to other urban or regional manufacturing complexes must at best be inferred from piecemeal data or through statistical estimations of expected interaction (e.g., Britton, Gilmour, Karaska).[1] Except in those cases where dependency is clearly demonstrated by such phenomena as shipments of raw materials from unifunctional sites to specific manufacturing complexes (Hodge and Wong)[2] the general problem of industrial interconnectivity is very difficult to assess with any degree of reliability. Solution of this problem is, however, important if a realistic assessment of the functional relationship between urban places and their hinterlands, or urban places and industrial enterprises in other urban spaces is to be made (e.g., Steed).[3] Assessment of the functional basis of any urban place is mandatory before realistic and productive policies and programs can be adopted and implemented to accomplish such objectives as economic stability or employment growth (Lever, Moseley and Townroe).[4]

Objectives

The general purpose of this paper is to describe and assess the Alberta provincial economy through examination of patterns of inter-industry linkages. Manufacturing linkages are specifically examined for evidence of (1) consumption of provincially-manufactured goods, (2) production of provincially-consumed products, and (3) the existence of a provincial manufacturing complex. This paper is directed toward those interested in the general academic study of regional manufacturing linkages, those concerned with the impact of resource-extraction on the structure of manufacturing in a sparsely-populated region, and those responsible for the development and implementation of economic development policies in Alberta.

Methodology

The objectives of this paper require measurement and description of the magnitude of provincial inter-industry linkages for individual Alberta manufacturing firms.[5] The value of provincial purchases and sales of manufactured goods were obtained from 503 Alberta firms. Each firm was also requested to provide an estimate of the extent to which it purchased commodities from, or made shipments to, Alberta manufacturers in six industrial groups. Composition of these six industrial categories was determined by the nature of commodities produced and by the general economic sector with which individual firms were associated. With only two minor exceptions-- synthetic textiles and agricultural machinery--the six industrial groups in this analysis are extensions of broad industrial categories and groupings found in the Standard Industrial Classification Code. The estimates by each firm of its linkage with firms in the six industrial groups have been aggregated to describe the provincial industrial linkages of Alberta manufacturers. Data limitations precluded application of such techniques as interregional input-output or linear programming analyses but the unique character of the data themselves offered insights into the general importance of provincial manufacturing linkages to Alberta firms which so far have not emanated from any other source.

Data Sources

Statistics Canada does not collect locational data related to inter-industry linkages during its annual census of manufacturing, but concentrates instead simply on the measurement of the magnitude of purchases, production, and sales (shipments) of individual firms. Data are published by areal statistical unit provided that they do not violate Statistics Canada's rules of confidentiality. Published data for manufacturers in Canada, however, do not contain information which permit spatial and locational assessment of inter-industry industrial relations. Published data do not permit analysis of individual firms and at best reveal some statis locational information about industries or sectors in selected places and regions if the rules of confidentiality are not endangered. The government itself seldom obtains industrial information on origin and destination of materials even for inhouse spatial research; furthermore, the rather voluminous but geographically sterile information contained in individual census returns is not commonly available to non-governmental researchers.

The investigator of inter-industry manufacturing linkages must obtain his own information. Most researchers seek data directly from personnel of key firms through such devices as questionnaires. This procedure is expensive, in money and time, both for the researcher and for industrial management. Few firms, if any, seem to maintain adequate information organized in a manner suitable for the geographer. Few manufacturers appear to know the specific origin of all their commodities; they do not maintain files to separate purchases of raw and manufactured goods, and they do not differentiate purchases by "neat" statistical areas such as metropolitan location or province. Many firms purchasing through such middle men as wholesalers are unable to identify either the original producer or even the country of origin of many commodities required. In Alberta, where many manufactured products are produced by assembly of items from diverse suppliers, few manufacturers can with certainty answer in general terms even the simplest questions posed by the industrial geographer if those questions pertain to origin and destination. Many entrepreneurs do not perceive industry in the same manner as the geographer and often refer to construction as an industry, or to retailing as an industry akin to those enterprises engaged in manufacturing. Many firms listed by Statistics Canada as manufacturers plead, when contacted, that they are primarily engaged in services such as repair and maintenance and undertake manufacturing only as an auxiliary and custom activity. In all cases, however, even when the entrepreneur is willing to assist with industrial research, his own files are usually inadequate to provide accurate spatial data.

Most manufacturers also appear to be victims of questionnaire-overkill. They are subjected to questionnaires from various federal, provincial, and local agencies to the point where some claim that they must employ an accountant simply to report data to official organizations. Many claim that the data they have supplied should be released by the government; others are disillusioned with all types of industrial economic research undertaken by government and related institutions because nothing positive seems to emanate from the statistics submitted. One of the biggest obstacles facing the industrial geographer when approaching the entrepreneur thus seems to be the plethora of demands for data made by government.

Spatial inter-industry linkage analyses of the manufacturing economy cannot proceed without the co-operation of industrial management. The data base of the present research--gathered as part of a general analysis of petroleum-generated manufacturing linkages in Alberta--was prepared from a short questionnaire sent to each manufacturer in Calgary who expressed an interest in the project during a preliminary telephone conversation. Since by late 1971, the Alberta Bureau of Statistics had almost completed its Census of Manufacturing for 1968 based on returns from questionnaires submitted to Alberta firms, the same firms were contacted by the authors during the summer of 1972 and asked to supply data for the year, 1968. The questionnaire survey provided data on approximately one-quarter of Alberta's manufacturing establishment.

Experience by other analysts suggested that most questionnaires prepared by industrial geographers and regional scientists not only ask for too much data, but ask questions which even the most willing respondent cannot answer. Many questionnaires also do not provide the respondent with any incentive to reply or to identify with the objectives of the research or the researchers. The questionnaire utilized in this study sought to overcome these objectives through brevity in the questions asked and through personal contact via the telephone to arouse the interest and sympathy of the person whose co-operation was essential if the questionnaire were to be returned.

The questionnaire sought sixteen pieces of information. Section one asked for the value of all manufactured goods purchased and shipped by the firm, the proportion of total purchases comprised by Alberta-produced commodities, and the proportion of total shipments which went to customers in Alberta. Section two asked the respondent to allocate the share of manufactured goods either purchased from, or shipped to, Alberta manufacturers according to six industrial categories. The types of industry comprising each category were contained on a sheet attached to the questionnaire. The entire population of manufacturers was contacted; sampling in the Alberta context could not yield meaningful results due to the small number of manufacturers in many industries. The questionnaire was mailed to each entrepreneur on the same day as he agreed by telephone to assist with the study. The questionnaire was introduced by a covering letter reiterating the objectives of the research and promising a summary of the research findings for each respondent. A self-addressed stamped return envelope accompanied each questionnaire. If the questionnaire was not returned within a month, the potential respondent was again contacted and where necessary was mailed another copy of the questionnaire. In the second phase of the general research program--not analysed in this paper--those firms which completed the questionnaire were approached in 1973 with a questionnaire designed to measure entrepreneurial attitudes toward the economic milieu of Alberta.

Data Reliability

How useful and reliable are the data obtained for this study? Most entrepreneurs seem to have provided the most recent annual data they had available and not that for 1968. Others responded with data for their own fiscal year. Hence, the years to which responses to questions 1 and 3 pertain vary within the study and may comprise all of, or part of, 1968, 1969, 1970 or 1971, or may extend from 1971 into 1972. The data at the best are probably reasonably accurate and do not vary considerably in quality from information derived from the questionnaires employed in the Census of Manufacturing. The responses to questions 2 and 4, and to all those in part II, clearly are "guesstimates"; no entrepreneur maintains the records or staff necessary to complete these questions precisely. These values must be accepted at face value and treated with great caution; they probably reflect the respondents' perception of the magnitude of his firm's inter-industry linkage as much as the real nature of product movement. Conclusions drawn from this study, therefore, are tentative and must be corroborated by similar studies in which uncertainty and inaccuracy are controlled and reduced. The data limitations will likely plague all such studies in Canada, however, until fundamental changes are made in the way entrepreneurs maintain their records, and government agencies collect and disseminate spatial economic data pertinent to the individual firm.

Experience in approaching Alberta manufacturers suggests that there is a definite limit to the quality and depth of information which a researcher can expect to obtain from the entrepreneur or manager. The simple questions asked in the questionnaire heavily taxed the ability of most firms to reply. Refinements to the type of inter-industry locational data which can be obtained probably should be made on the questionnaire forms of the annual census of manufacturing; data provided on purchases and shipments should be accompanied by the location of supplier and consumer. However, even this refinement would probably not benefit the independent researcher because it would compound the problem of confidentiality and corporate security. In a general survey such as that conducted for this study, the problem of obtaining inter-industry locational data is probably unresolvable in our society. Some investigators have overcome certain handicaps by concentrating on one industrial sector such as mobile homes or iron and steel where in-depth interviewing can be conducted and where more information is available as part of the general knowledge about the industry in trade literature, etc. The smaller number of firms involved in most specific studies also lessens the cost in time and money involved with obtaining data.

The questionnaire used in the study was purposefully very specific in its objectives. The questionnaire did not seek information on the share of purchased manufactured goods in the total value of all materials purchased by the firm. Although this information would be interesting to analyze in other studies, it would not greatly enhance our understanding of Alberta's inter-industry manufacturing linkages and would probably lessen the willingness of the entrepreneur to provide any information because it would lengthen the questionnaire. Similarly, information on the extent to which commodity shipments are comprised of goods purchased or goods of own manufacture was not requested. The questionnaire also did not ascertain the extent to which the firm was engaged in activities other than manufacturing, or the number or range of commodities produced in any establishment.

RELATED STUDIES

Analyses of Linkage

Many of the general problems and achievements related to studies of inter-industry linkage and external economies have been reviewed by such authors as Britton,[6] Karaska,[7] Richter,[8] Streit,[9] Gilmour,[10] and most recently, Czamanski,[11] and Schmidt.[12] Wilbur Thompson[13] has provided a lucid and succinct review of the processes of internal economic growth generally associated with urban places. Most discussions of linkage and external economies suggest furthermore that shortcomings in statistical data will continue to plague analysts for the foreseeable future. While considerable gains have been made in understanding regional inter-industry linkages, and in appreciating some of the general relationships between linkage and agglomeration or external economies (Beyers,[14] Campbell,[15] Moseley,[16] Lever,[17]) inter-industry linkages at the level of the firm are still relatively few in number and have largely been confined to studies of firms in particular industries (Hodge and Wong,[18] Steed,[19] Schmidt,[20] Taylor,[21] and Hamilton[22]) in localities where the existence of manufacturing industries and industrial complexes has long been recognized although perhaps not adequately researched and analyzed.

Studies of inter-industry linkages at the level of the firm have been confined also to industries whose backward and forward industrial material relations could be reasonably determined from private and public sources. Functional cohesion within industries in processes and products appears to be a prime requisite if meaningful statements are to be made on the influence of size, product mix, ownership and productivity on material linkage networks among manufacturing enterprises (Schmidt).[23]

Studies, however, of inter-industry material linkages among firms in weakly-developed urban-industrial regions in which the majority of firms purchase materials directly or indirectly from extra-regional suppliers, or in which the bulk of final local demand for industrial commodities is directly supplied by extra-regional

42

producers, do not comprise a sizable share of the current literature. In other words, studies of manufacturing at the level of
the firm have in their recent formative period primarily been concerned with industries and regions in which the magnitude of manufacturing employment and production were important phenomena. The
examination of firms' manufacturing linkages in other regions, such
as resource-extractive regions with heavy emphasis on the export of
unprocessed commodities, has not received adequate attention despite the obvious implications of such research for notions of
regional development, diversification, and urban stability. Thompson has observed that, despite the quantification of flows among
given sets of local industries in local input-output tables, planners and economic geographers still do not have "the full development equivalent, a locational matrix that tells us which industries
follow a given industry to a locality and when."[24] The concomitant
of this observation, made by Thompson in a slightly different context, is that examination of the timing of growth, development,
and functional expansion is necessary if we are to evaluate "the
process by which structural change takes place in the local indus-
try-mix"[25] and to confirm either the development of local agglomeration economies and regional externalities, or the relative growth
and dominance of residentiary industries in face of the decline of
the original propulsive primary industry.

Research in Alberta

A recent review of studies of the Alberta economy contains
few references to other analyses of material flows among sectors of
the provincial economy.[26] The one input-output analysis completed
for the province, by Wright[27] on the basis of 1962 data, demonstrated the close similarity between the impact of petroleum and
agriculture on the provincial economy; two of the strongest sectors
of the Alberta manufacturing economy relate to the processing of
agricultural commodities, and to the production of primary metals,
engineering, and transportation equipment for eventual consumption
by the petroleum industry or by activities generated from the growth
of the primary petroleum industry.[28] His study analyzes all
economic flows through the provincial economy, and also estimates
provincial export and import of commodities. Wright's report,
furthermore, adds a perspective to the present study by presenting
manufacturing flows as part of the aggregate contribution of primary and secondary industry, and the "service industries" (which
obviously includes tertiary and quaternary functions). A major
problem in completing adapting the manufacturing flows in Wright's
matrixes to the needs of the industrial geographer in Alberta
arises in attempts to distinguish the consumption of imports by
Alberta manufacturers from those by other provincial consumers;
similarly, the extent to which exports arise with the manufacturing economy as compared to the other provincial producers cannot
be determined from his matrix.

43

Despite the work of Alberta analysts such as E.J. Hanson[29] few studies of the spatial impact of petroleum on the Alberta regional and urban economy have been carried out. Entries in a recent review of urban and regional studies in Alberta for the period 1950-1974 suggest that the impact of petroleum--the dominant growth sector in the provincial economy throughout this period--on the spatial structure of the economy has either been considered unworthy of investigation, or so minor as not to warrant serious study. With few exceptions, geographers and economists alike have ignored the spatial structure of Alberta's resource-based economy. Drugge[30] has specifically examined some of the locational requirements of energy-intensive industries of Alberta. Peter Smith's[31] work on Fort Saskatchewan and Calgary stands alone in its concern for the changing industrial composition of two important urban economies. The changing provincial distribution of manufacturing has been analyzed in short papers by Leigh and Carter[32] and Seifried;[33] Barr[34] has considered Alberta's industrial diversification as part of his analyses of post-World War II economic change in the three prairie provinces. Theses on the subject of petroleum-generated industrial location have been confined to analyses by Zieber[35] of the location of oil offices in Edmonton and Calgary, by Curtis[36] of the generation of tertiary industrial linkages in Edmonton with the petroleum industry, and by Wilson[37] of some of the factors attracting manufacturing to Alberta.

The rather weakly developed portfolio of existing analyses and the narrow profile of their interests have led the present authors to prepare this report on Alberta with data gathered during research into petroleum-generated manufacturing linkages within the Albertan economy.

MANUFACTURING IN ALBERTA

Alberta's Manufacturing Structure

The diverse structure of Alberta's manufacturing economy suggests that strong intra-industry absorption of locally produced manufactured commodities is not one of the region's prime characteristics. Alberta, located on the periphery of national and international manufacturing complexes, lacks sufficient local or regional demand to stimulate a wide variety of strong intra-regional manufacturing linkages of its own but has generated significant production chains with extra-regional producers. Regional resource extraction, however, has generated limited local manufacturing chains. Alberta and other Canadian regions take advantage of mobile external economies in their backward linkages with extra-regional producers serving national and international markets or depending on local access to numerous related producers. These characteristics help account for the general absence--except for a narrow profile of petrochemical and wood industries--from Alberta of those

44

manufacturing establishments whose output is characterized by large volumes of standardized commodities, and whose manufacturing producers depend on the mass assembly of numerous manufactured subcomponents.

Alberta, however, displays reasonably strong manufacturing linkages among producers of perishable agricultural commodities prior to shipment to final regional and extra-regional markets, and has significant linkages among firms related to the production of custom goods or small-run items for resource-development, and industrial and residential construction. Such manufacturers continue to rely for many standardized products on manufacturers in extra-regional industrial complexes such as the Quebec City-Windsor industrial corridor.

The number of manufacturing establishments in Alberta is dominated by those engaged in non-food, general manufacturing, and food and beverage production which comprise over one-half of the provincial total; these two groups together with food, paper, and allied industries account for three-quarters of all Alberta manufacturing establishments (Table I). Non-food and general manufacturing industries are more numerous in Edmonton and Calgary, however, whereas manufacturers in the other two leading groups are found more frequently in intermediate and smaller urban places, i.e., in greater general proximity to the location of primary industry such as agriculture and forestry. Manufacturers most clearly identified with production of petroleum and petroleum-related products in Alberta, however—primary metal, engineering, transportation, and petrochemical industries—comprise less than one-fifth of the number of manufacturing establishments in Alberta but are most heavily concentrated of all manufacturing establishments in the two major cities, Edmonton and Calgary.

When manufacturing in Alberta is measured according to the criterion, "value added during manufacturing," however, the dominant industrial group in the province is food and beverage production; according to this criterion, the petrochemical group also assumes an important share in the provincial economy but producers in the non-food and general manufacturing group no longer appear so significant as when their importance is measured according to number of establishments.

Producers in the primary metal and engineering group, however, make approximately the same contribution to the provincial economy regardless which of the three criteria in Table I is used to measure them. The value of factory shipments, however, clearly indicates the overall importance of food and beverage producers to the generation of manufacturing wealth in Alberta, and the important contribution to provincial industrial income of the two groups related to the petroleum industry—members of the primary metal,

TABLE I

ALBERTA: STRUCTURE OF MANUFACTURING – 1970

INDUSTRIAL GROUP	Establishments No.	%	Value Added $x10^6	%	Shipments $x10^6	%	CALGARY AND EDMONTON Establishments No.	%	Value Added $x10^6	%	Shipments $x10^6	%	RELATIVE SHARE OF CALGARY AND EDMONTON IN ALBERTA MANUFACTURING, BY INDUSTRIAL GROUP % of Establishments	% of Value Added	% of Shipments
1. Food & Beverage	463	24	185.	27	764.	40	180	17	131	28	483	38	39	71	63
2. Petrochemical, Coal & Synthetic Textile	93	5	114.	17	318.	17	79	7	65	14	246	20	85	57	77
3. Non-food, and General Manufacturing	592	30	117.	17	204.	11	439	40	97	21	170	14	74	83	83
4. Wood, Paper, and Allied Industries	374	19	77.	11	168.	9	92	8	35	8	79	6	25	45	47
5. Primary Metal, Engineering, Transportation Industries	324	16	134.	19	347.	18	251	23	93	20	205	16	77	69	59
6. Non-Metallic Mineral Products	110	6	63.	9	102.	5	52	5	45	9	73	6	47	71	72
TOTAL	1956	100	690.	100	1903.	100	1093	100	466	100	1256	100	56	68	66

SOURCE: Industry and Resources 1973. Alberta Bureau of Statistics, Alberta Industry and Commerce, 1973, pp. 25-33; Missing data have been estimated from other sources.

engineering, transportation and petrochemical groups. Except for
manufactuerds in the wood and paper group, producers in all other
groups when measured according to value of factory shipments are
heavily concentrated in Edmonton and Calgary which in manufacturing
clearly dominate the secondary industrial distribution pattern in
Alberta. In summary, the data in Table I show that, in the production of manufacturing wealth, Alberta's manufacturing economy is
heavily influenced by food and beverage, petrochemical, primary
metal, engineering and transportation industries; and the spatial
location of most manufacturing, whether measured by value added or
factory shipments, is heavily influenced by Edmonton and Calgary.

The distribution of returns from our 1972 questionnaire
survey--the basis of analysis in this paper--is reasonably close to
the distribution of establishments among the six industrial groups
in Alberta (Table II). The survey returns slightly underemphasize
the food, beverage, wood, paper and allied industries (members of
groups 1 and 4) but more than adequately represent the two most
diverse industrial groups, non-food and general manufacturing (group
3) and primary metal, engineering and transportation (group 5). In
all cases, however, the survey obtained returns from at least ten
per cent of the members in any industrial group and coincidentally
had the most satisfactory returns from the most complex or technologically complicated industrial groups. The distribution of
survey returns among industrial groups, however, is almost identical
with the distribution of establishments among the six industrial
groups of Edmonton and Calgary (Table I). Of the 503 returns cited
in Table II, 382 or 76% are from establishments in Calgary and
Edmonton. The authors feel, therefore, that data obtained in the
questionnaire survey adequately represent sectorially the composition
of the Alberta manufacturing economy although Calgary and Edmonton
are slightly over-represented in the spatial structure of the survey.

Provincial Commodity Shipments

Recently published data pertinent to provincial shipments of
manufactured goods show that the Alberta food and beverage industry
ships just over half of its goodsto consumers in Alberta and satis-
fies two-thirds of the demand for these products in the province
(Table III). The Alberta food and beverage industries, therefore,
have major extra-regional markets which suggest that this industrial
group has strong forward linkages with consumers outside of Alberta.
This same general relationship holds for the petrochemical and wood
and paper industries. Clearly these manufacturers located in Alberta, while not producing the full range of goods necessary to
supply the total regional demand for these products, do nevertheless have strong regional and extra-regional forward linkages.
The data do not, however, indicate if these shipments were made to
other manufacturers or to consumers in other sectors of the economy.
Such disaggregated spatial flow data are not available from

47

TABLE II.

ALBERTA MANUFACTURING STRUCTURE REPRESENTED BY DATA FROM

QUESTIONNAIRE SURVEY, 1972

INDUSTRIAL GROUP	ESTABLISHMENTS		
	No.	% of Survey Total	% of 1970 Actual Group Total
1. FOOD AND BEVERAGE	89	18	19
2. PETROCHEMICAL, COAL, & SYNTHETIC TEXTILE	23	4	25
3. NON-FOOD, & GENERAL MANUFACTURING	190	38	32
4. WOOD, PAPER & ALLIED INDUSTRIES	36	7	10
5. PRIMARY METAL, ENGINEERING, TRANSPORTATION INDUSTRIES	134	27	41
6. NON-METALLIC MINERAL PRODUCTS	31	6	10
TOTAL	503	100	26*

* Total number of establishments represented by the questionnaire survey as a percent of all manufacturing establishments in Alberta, 1970 as reported in Industry and Resources 1973. Alberta Bureau of Statistics, Alberta Industry and Commerce, 1973, pp. 25-33.
SOURCE: Questionnaire Survey, May-August, 1972.

TABLE III.

SHIPMENTS OF GOODS OF OWN MANUFACTURE (1967)

| INDUSTRIAL GROUP | SHIPMENTS BY ALBERTA MANUFACTURERS: | | | | SHIPMENTS TO ALBERTA BY ALL CANADIAN MANUFACTURERS (3) |
	(1) TO ALBERTA $x10^6	(1) as % of (2)	(1) as % of (3)	(2) TOTAL TO ALL CUSTOMERS* $x10^6	$x10^6
1. FOOD & BEVERAGE	345.	54	67	642.	512.
2. PETROCHEMICAL, COAL & SYNTHETIC TEXTILE	156.	55	49	282.	318.
3. NON-FOOD, & GENERAL MANUFACTURING	85.	65	19	132.	439.
4. WOOD, PAPER, & ALLIED INDUSTRIES	67.	48	45	139.	151.
5. PRIMARY METAL, ENGINEERING, TRANSPORTATION INDUSTRIES	159.	66	34	240.	463.
6. NON-METALLIC MINERAL PRODUCTS	72.	78	85	92.	85.
TOTAL	884.	58	45	1,527.	1,968.

SOURCE: "Destination of Total Shipments of Goods of Own Manufacture, 1967", Destination of Shipments of Manufacturers, Catalogue 31-504 Occasional, Information Canada 1971, Table 2; Industry and Resources 1973. Alberta Bureau of Statistics, Alberta Industry and Commerce, 1973, p. 18. Missing data have been estimated.

* Includes customers in foreign countries.

government and must be obtained through questionnaire surveys.

Nearly two-thirds of the output of the primary metal, engineering, and transportation equipment industries is destined for provincial consumption; surprisingly, however, Alberta manufacturers supply only one-third of the total provincial demand for these manufactured goods. Although extra-regional supply of automobiles probably reduces the significance of the Alberta manufacturers to total consumption of goods to this group, the export destinations of most commodities manufactured by industries in this industrial group is chiefly confined to adjacent Canadian political regions.

Alberta manufacturers engaged in non-food and general manufacturing, and production of non-metallic mineral products ship the majority of their commodities to provincial consumers; these same manufacturers, however, vary in the extent to which they satisfy the total provincial demand for commodities produced by firms in their industrial groups. Producers in the non-metallic mineral industries seem to enjoy a protected market due to the generally high friction of distance associated with their commodities, the provincial availability of necessary raw materials, and the ability of regional demand to support economic enterprises and scales of output in these industries. General and non-food manufacturers, however, while shipping a major share of their product to provincial consumers satisfy less than one-fifth of the total provincial demand for commodities produced by this industrial group.

This dichotomy—while not the focus of this paper—probably is related to such factors as size of local market, general economies of scale—both internal and external—operating within the industries of this group, and general comparative advantages held by producers in those major Canadian and foreign industrial regions which ship goods to Alberta.

ALBERTA MANUFACTURING LINKAGES

The questionnaire responses permit, for the first time, meaningful although tentative empirically-derived statements to be made about many aspects of Alberta's manufacturing linkages. The value of shipments made by respondents in each industrial group comprise a significant share of the total value of shipment by these groups published by Statistics Canada. Clearly the size of industrial production of those who responded to the questionnaire is sufficient to expect the patterns of industrial linkage reasonably to reflect patterns for all manufacturers in Alberta.

Aggregate Backward and Forward Linkages

The strongest backward linkages are evidenced by food and beverage industries, and by non-metallic mineral producers (Table IV).

50

TABLE IV.

AGGREGATE INDUSTRIAL LINKAGES OF ALBERTA MANUFACTURING PLANTS

| INDUSTRIAL GROUP | PURCHASE OF MANUFACTURED MATERIALS AND SUPPLIES | | | | | SELLING VALUE OF FACTORY SHIPMENTS | | | | | |
| | TOTAL PURCHASE: | | FROM ALBERTA MANUFACTURERS: | | ALBERTA PURCHASES AS A PERCENT OF TOTAL PURCHASES BY INDUSTRIAL GROUP | TOTAL SHIPMENTS: | | SHIPMENTS WITHIN ALBERTA: | | ALBERTA SHIPMENTS AS A PERCENT OF TOTAL SHIPMENTS BY INDUSTRIAL GROUP |
	NO. OF ESTABLISHMENTS	VALUE $x10^6$	NO. OF ESTABLISHMENTS	VALUE $x10^6$		NO. OF ESTABLISHMENTS	VALUE $x10^6$	NO. OF ESTABLISHMENTS	VALUE $x10^6$	
1. FOOD & BEVERAGE	89	36.3	81	23.7	65	89	300.0	85	127.1	42
2. PETROCHEMICAL, COAL, & SYNTHETIC TEXTILE	23	20.5	18	3.5	17	23	98.8	23	39.2	40
3. NON-FOOD, AND GENERAL MANUFACTURING	190	56.8	139	4.6	8	190	146.4	189	80.8	55
4. WOOD, PAPER, AND ALLIED INDUSTRIES	36	26.6	33	6.2	23	36	60.7	36	34.2	56
5. PRIMARY METAL, ENGINEERING TRANSPORTATION INDUSTRIES	134	125.9	118	21.3	17	134	212.6	132	138.6	65
6. NON-METALLIC MINERAL PRODUCTS	31	15.7	28	8.9	57	31	40.2	31	31.3	78
TOTAL	503	281.8	417	68.3	24	503	858.7	496	451.2	52

SOURCE: questionnaire survey, May-August, 1972.

Producers in these industries rely heavily on semi-processed goods and on packaging materials in the form of paper, paperboard, plastics, glass, etc. Edmonton's petro-chemical industry similarly makes significant local purchases of packaging materials but the relatively weak backward manufacturing linkages appear to reflect its purchase of chemical bases and related materials from producers outside of Alberta.

The remaining three groups also exhibit weak backward manufacturing linkages within the province. Non-food and general manufacturing industries clearly rely on sub-components produced in central Canada and foreign industrial regions. These Edmonton manufacturers are at the end of the production chain and are assembling manufactured goods for sale to the final consumer. Alberta's economy in this respect must clearly be described as consumer-oriented (to personal or industrial consumers). Wood, paper and allied industries also rely heavily on lumber and paper from outside the province. Glues and inks originate from elsewhere. The strength of linkage would be greater if Alberta had a finished paper industry but at the time of the survey, the province had only one pulp mill, the primary product of which is shipped entirely outside the province for conversion into paper. The major Alberta purchases of manufactured goods by these industries appear to be for commodities which do not directly enter into the production process or comprise a real share of the final product. Enterprises engaged in primary metals, engineering, and transportation also purchase a major share of their manufactured goods outside the province but are different from firms in group 2 because the supply of components to the engineering and transportation industries probably means that goods purchased within the province do enter into the final product of these producers and are not adjunct to the main manufacturing process. However, the backward linkages of groups 3 and 5 reveal how dependent Alberta is on manufacturing processes and enterprises in other parts of Canada or the world.

Although the proportion of manufactured goods purchased within Alberta varies from one group to another, most establishments in Alberta appear to make some purchase of manufactured goods within Alberta. In all groups except non-food and general manufacturing, nearly all respondents to the survey reported making some purchase within Alberta. Non-food and general manufacturing firms have the weakest backward links with provincial manufacturers, and many of them make no significant purchases at all of goods manufactured within Alberta.

While most respondents were able to identify the extent to which they purchased goods from Alberta manufacturers, many were unable to determine the extent to which manufacturers, as opposed to all consumers, consumed their products because so many of their commodities were marketed through wholesalers and agencies. The questionnaire sought, therefore, to determine the extent to which sales were made to any customers in Alberta. The data in Table IV, however, appear at first to suggest that the linkage between Alberta manufacturers and consumers--forward linkages--involves more firms than those associated with backward linkages. All but seven respondents reported making some shipment to Alberta customers but, when data from part II of the questionnaire were analyzed for evidence of shipments to Alberta manufacturers, only 206 out of 503 respondents provided evidence that they shipped to manufacturers. Thus, the number of firms reporting backward linkages--417--is far greater than the number making shipments to Alberta manufacturers. Many Alberta manufacturers comprise the last link of the production chain; nearly three-fifths of the firms surveyed were engaged in production of goods for final Alberta consumption, either by the public or various non-manufacturing sectors of the provincial economy.

Five groups represented in the last column in Table IV (survey data) differ by 1-15% from data for those groups shown in column 2 of Table III (published data for 1967). The figures for group 6 are identical--78%--and for group 5 almost identical--65% and 66% respectively. At least two possible interpretations can be made of these similarities and differences.

In the first case, we could argue that, since the data are for two different time periods, they indicate (1) that non-metallic mineral producers, generally manufacturing low-value, high weight goods, continue to suffer from a high friction of distance on their output, (2) that primary metal, engineering and transportation industries in Alberta have reached a relatively static situation in which most of their output is provincially consumed although with the recent growth in northern petroleum exploration Alberta producers of these commodities should be starting to divert a larger share of their output to consumers north of the province, (3) that Alberta is increasing its role as a producer of food and beverages, petrochemical products and general manufactured items for extra-regional consumers, and (4) that Alberta is shipping a greater share of wood, paper, and allied products to provincial consumers perhaps in response to greater demand within the province for packaging materials, structural lumber and general wood building materials.

On the other hand, a somewhat different interpretation of the differences and similarities between the two sets of figures could suggest (1) that the questionnaire survey employed to compile Table IV was biased in groups 1 and 3 toward larger enterprises which rely more heavily on extra-regional markets than their smaller counterparts, (2) that any variation in the composition of response between the two surveys by the relatively few members of the petrochemical, coal and synthetic textile group would amost certainly cause the figures to be different, (3) that the 1972 data do not incorporate figures for the Hinton pulp mill--which ships almost its entire product outside Alberta, and (4) that, since both sets of data are based on surveys, some chance variation between the data sets is bound to occur due to survey error, etc. Although it would be foolhardy within the realm of industrial geography to make hard and fast statements about the specific accuracy of any survey data, and although published statistics by their formality appear to be more trustworthy, the authors submit that the ability of government to obtain accurate information from entrepreneurs is not necessarily greater than that of the academic researcher due to the antipathy of many entrepreneurs toward the ever-increasing demands by government for data, and due to the personal contact which the authors in this case had with so many Alberta entrepreneurs who appeared to identify closely with the aims of the research.

On this basis, the first of the two cases presented is reasonable and probably reflects (1) Alberta's important manufacturing role in satisfying regional and extra-regional demand for food, beverage, petrochemical, wood and allied products, (2) the existence within the province of market-oriented producers of diverse commodities for petroleum exploration and development, and (3) the operation of numerous and diverse manufacturers of light industrial commodities for the public sector, for construction industries, and for personal consumers. Finally producers in group 6 seem to be fulfilling a rather normal role of market-orientation due to the nature of their products.

What do the differences between the relative strengths of the backward and forward provincial manufacturing linkages of each group in Table IV suggest about the secondary industrial structure of Alberta? Forward linkages are approximately twice as important relatively than backward linkages; Alberta manufacturers purchase approximately one-quarter of their manufactured inputs from provincial producers whereas they ship approximately half of their output to customers within the province. Alberta clearly is highly dependent for goods manufactured by groups 2, 3, 4 and 5 on extra-regional enterprises. On the other hand, except for groups 1 and 2 which ship two-fifths of their output to regional customers, the other producers in this set ship between one-half and two-thirds of their output to provincial customers. Non-metallic mineral producers are strongly linked in both directions with regional manufacturers, and food and beverage producers clearly have strong regional backward links with manufacturers but rely heavily on extra-regional markets.

Although the relative importance of provincial sales is greater than provincial purchases a great many more firms engage in provincial backward linkages than forward linkages with Alberta manufacturers; since 417 manufacturers bought from Alberta manufacturers, whereas only 206 sold to manufacturers, Alberta generally is producing goods for the final provincial consumer and is not characterized by manufacturers primarily engaged in buying from or selling to each other. Over three-fifths of shipments of manufactured goods within the province are destined for non-manufacturers. The Alberta economy is really part of manufacturing complexes or systems in other regions of Canada or the world; Alberta producers are largely at the end of the production chain, the prior links of which are not found primarily in Alberta.

Although the number of backward linkages exceeds that of forward linkages with provincial manufacturers by a factor of two to one, the dollar value of shipments to Alberta manufacturers, $283 million is approximately four times greater than the value of backward linkages. The number of provincial backward linkages of Alberta manufacturers is high but the average dollar value of purchases is low; the average value of forward provincial linkages is approximately eight times greater than that of provincial backward linkage. Although Alberta's relatively weak provincial backward linkage is not intuitively unexpected, the province's general reliance on extra-provincial sales of its manufactured goods for approximately one-half of all sales of these goods prevents the provincial manufacturing economy from being unequivocally labelled as a regional producer of manufactured goods. The data presented in Tables IV and III suggest that both enquiries, the former in 1972 and the latter in 1967, have identified a strong component in the provincial manufacturing economy which is dependent on extra-regional sales.

Although the overall economic function of Alberta might show strong signs of governmental and business administration, regional provision of petroleum services, and production of crude petroleum and natural gas, the provincial manufacturing sector, due to food and beverages, petrochemicals, non-food and general manufacturing, and wood, paper and allied industries, is far from being excessively dependent on the Alberta market.

Inter-Industry Backward and Forward Linkages

Alberta firms are most closely linked in their purchase of provincially-manufactured goods with the food, beverage, primary metal, engineering and transportation industries; approximately two-thirds of the value of backward linkages is with these two industrial groups. The strong provincial reliance on industrial groups 1 and 5 is consistent with the basic importance of agriculture and petroleum as the main generators of industrial production in Alberta. The figures in Table V clearly demonstrate that the influence of these two basic economic sectors not only is manifested in input-output analyses but also is present in the form of inter-industry linkages among downstream manufacturers. The manufacturing economy of Alberta, however, bears almost no direct relation to the manufacture of petroleum-based commodities in which previously manufactured petroleum commodities serve as the basic raw materials. The figures in Table V suggest

55

TABLE V

INTER-GROUP PURCHASES OF MANUFACTURED COMMODITIES WITHIN ALBERTA
BY ALBERTA MANUFACTURERS

(% of Total Purchases, by each group, of Commodities Manufactured
within Alberta)

INDUSTRIAL GROUP	FROM	1	2	3	4	5	6	TOTAL PURCHASES $x10^6
BY								
1		41.4	1.9	10.2	31.9	10.8	3.8	23.7
2		2.0	36.6	12.1	17.6	23.7	8.0	3.5
3		N	8.0	30.0	30.5	29.1	2.2	4.6
4		N	20.1	16.1	46.5	11.8	5.3	6.2
5		N	1.9	15.5	14.4	64.9	3.3	21.3
6		N	3.8	3.9	11.4	19.3	61.6	8.9
PURCHASES BY ALL GROUPS		14.5	6.0	13.0	24.2	30.8	11.5	68.3

N = Negligible

SOURCE: Questionnaire Survey, May-August 1972.

that those industries processing agricultural commodities and those
manufacturing oilfield and construction equipment, for example, engage in important inter-industry transfers of industrial commodities
whereas those engaged in all other industrial groups do not.

Perhaps it is unreasonable to expect the Alberta petrochemical industry to play a large role as a supplier to provincial manufacturers given the small regional population and the great distances
to North American and world industrial and consumer markets. Locational inertia caused by such factors as existing population and
industrial distribution in Canada and the "headstart" in manufacturing possessed by producers in Ontario and Quebec--as well as their
more advantageous spatial access to international markets--obviously
must have some great bearing on the relative underdevelopment of
petroleum-generated manufacturing linkages in Alberta. While we
have not measured the significance of petroleum as a *raw material* to
oil refineries, for example, or natural gas to fertilizer complexes,
and connot comment, therefore, on the extent to which petroleum is
converted by primary manufacturing establishments into relatively
unsophisticated products such as gasoline and fertilizer, the linkage patterns in Table V do show that few Alberta firms have any
meaningful backward linkages with the petrochemical industry. One
of the obvious implications of this observation is that growth, decline or even demise of the conventional provincial petroleum

industry will not directly affect to any sizeable extent the pattern
of backward manufacturing linkages--even by group 2--by Alberta manufacturers although curtailment of demand for oilfield and related
construction and transport equipment would affect industries in
group 5.

Inter-group linkages often imply that all members of the
group behave more or less in the same manner. However, the number
of establishments engaged in inter-group purchases clearly is not
consistent within all groups. The data in Table VI suggest that

TABLE VI.

NUMBER OF ALBERTA MANUFACTURING ESTABLISHMENTS ENGAGED IN
INTER-GROUP PURCHASES OF COMMODITIES MANUFACTURED WITHIN
ALBERTA

(Number of establishments analyzed: 503)

INDUSTRIAL GROUP							Number of establishments making:	
							Some Alberta Inter-group Purchase	No Alberta Inter-group Purchase
	FROM	1	2	3	4	5	6	
BY								
1		63	22	31	46	30	15	81	8
2		3	15	10	9	10	10	18	5
3		4	40	74	88	46	20	139	51
4		2	8	13	28	12	7	33	3
5		2	21	57	48	85	16	118	16
6		2	8	9	14	16	24	28	3
TOTAL		76	114	194	233	199	92	417	86

SOURCE: Questionnaire Survey, May-August, 1972

some firms in any group probably have a much greater connection with
Alberta producers than that of other firms in the group. This observation further suggests that the necessity to group manufacturers into only six groups has probably masked some important variations
which exist between individual enterprises and firms. The groups are
not internally homogeneous in terms of their linkages with other
Alberta firms. Many Alberta enterprises are small and many belong to
firms which have plants in other regions of Canada or in other countries. Diverse patterns of ownership, control, functional subordina-
tion, as well as important intra-group product differences, appear
to add to the heterogencous nature of Alberta's manufacturing linkages.

Any projection or recommendation for industrial policy or
strategy based on patterns derived for these six industrial groups

for example, must only proceed after careful scrutiny of the internal consistency of each group. This observation also suggests that consistent approaches in industrial development strategy in such a province as Alberta where there are relatively few firms in each industrial category must either be so general as to be specifically ineffective, or must deal with each firm on the basis of its own merits. On the other hand, the diversity of manufacturing in Alberta suggests that policies and programs in the national interest should be pursued in which the welfare of individual enterprises or firms in any region is enhanced by simultaneous solution of the problems of all members of any one industry in the small national Canadian economy. The diversity in linkage patterns in Table VI suggests furthermore that specific measures to aid such manufacturers in Alberta if repeated for themselves by other provincial governments, could adversely affect national industrial performance.

Although Alberta manufacturers generally have their strongest provincial backward linkages with firms in their own industrial group (Table V), their strongest forward provincial linkages--except for group 1--are almost entirely with firms outside their own industrial group (Table VII). Furthermore, with the exception of primary metal, engineering, and transportation equipment industries, Alberta manufacturers have the strongest component of their provincial sales to non-manufacturers. The patterns in Table VII enhance

TABLE VII.

INTER-GROUP ALBERTA SALES OF MANUFACTURED COMMODITIES BY ALBERTA MANUFACTURERS

INDUSTRIAL GROUP	TO	1	2	3	4	5	6	To Non-manufacturers	TOTAL SALES $x10^6$
BY									
1		25.2	N	N	N	---	---	74.5	127.1
2		N	5.0	12.4	3.6	10.0	---	69.0	39.2
3		2.4	9.1	4.5	4.3	4.3	.9	74.5	80.8
4		12.0	.5	6.2	9.3	.5	.5	71.0	34.2
5		5.3	23.3	5.3	1.0	22.9	2.2	40.0	138.6
6		10.6	1.2	3.4	.9	12.2	3.1	68.6	31.3
SALES BY ALL GROUPS		10.8	9.3	4.3	2.2	9.5	1.1	62.8	451.2

N = Negligible

SOURCE: QUESTIONNAIRE SURVEY, MAY-AUGUST, 1972.

the observation that Alberta manufacturers are indeed producing for
the final consumer—industrial or personal—and are engaged in producing a diverse range of commodities for provincial manufacturers.
The forward manufacturing linkage of food and beverage industries
is quite clearly with producers of commodities such as agricultural
feedstocks and livestock products, and semi-finished food and ani-
mal products for further processing prior to shipment to the final
individual consumer. Forward industrial linkage of the petrochemical industry is chiefly with the primary metal, engineering, transportation equipment and general manufacturing industries to satisfy
their demand for such commodities as petroleum-based lubricants and
chemicals. Non-food and general manufacturing industries in this
study are so diverse in function and product mix that, they as a
group satisfy some demand in every industrial group although their
major function is to produce items for final consumption by the individual consumer. Many products of this industrial group, therefore, might be seen as performing some auxiliary function in manufacturing enterprises rather than as entering the composition of
the commodities produced.

Output of the wood, paper and allied industry group clearly
consists of packaging materials and paper and wood products which
are consumed in numerous industrial and operational functions. This
industrial group supplies a diverse range of products to itself, to
the food and beverage industry, and to the general and non-food light
manufacturers of Alberta. Industrial group five, primary metals,
engineering, and transportation equipment, has the strongest linkage
with other Alberta manufacturers of all groups shown in Table VII.
This group may be thought of in the Alberta context as the most industrial of all in that most of its commodities do not go directly
to the final consumer without further manufacture. This industrial
group offers the strongest evidence of all groups that Alberta has
at least one manufacturing component which feeds the processing
lines of other manufacturers and creates industrial, as opposed to
service, multipliers within the province. If one of the criteria
for recognizing an industrial complex is that most of the output
should go to other manufacturers and not to final demand, then in
terms of forward linkage, the only group offering unequivocal evidence of some intra-provincial industrial complex associated with
Alberta's manufacturing output is that associated with primary metals,
engineering and transportation equipment. The total sales of this
group are larger than those of any other group and, because of their
prime orientation toward provincial manufacturers, reduce the total
value of the province's reliance on sales to non-manufacturers to
slightly over 60%.

Alberta's forward linkages as its backward ones are diverse
within each industrial group (Table VIII). Establishments in each
group generally ship some commodity to firms throughout the range of
groups; but all groups are similar in terms of the large number of

59

TABLE VIII.

NUMBER OF ALBERTA MANUFACTURING ESTABLISHMENTS ENGAGED IN INTER-GROUP SHIPMENTS
TO ALBERTA MANUFACTURERS

(Number of Establishments Analyzed: 503)

INDUSTRIAL GROUP									Number of Establishments making:	
								To Non-Manufacturers	Some Alberta Inter-group Shipments	No Alberta Shipments
	TO	1	2	3	4	5	6			
BY										
1		21	2	4	3	--	--	62	23	4
2		1	7	11	6	5	--	8	15	--
3		34	38	55	35	43	22	115	74	1
4		4	2	5	8	2	2	24	12	--
5		23	35	34	18	45	17	59	73	2
6		4	2	5	2	3	6	22	9	--
TOTAL		87	86	114	72	98	47	290	206	7

SOURCE: Questionnaire Survey, May-August, 1972.

firms which ship to non-manufacturers in the province. The only group where shipments to manufacturers clearly outweigh shipments to non-manufacturers in any major way--the number of firms in the petrochemical groups is very small although the ratio of shipments to manufacturers compared to those of non-manufacturers is high-- is associated with primary metals, engineering, and transportation equipment.

Although the value of linkages among firms may not be particularly outstanding in terms of major industrial regions, the number of enterprises engaged in some form of inter-industry shipment attests to the widespread influence of inter-industry sales among Alberta's manufacturers. Although Alberta is spatially separated from major industrial regions of North America, and although its aggregate contribution to national value added through manufacturing is very low, inter-industry linkages do nevertheless play an important role in the economy; peripheral economic regions such as Alberta may not be so industrially unsophisticated as their general role in agriculture, administration, supply, and resource extraction at first suggest. Perhaps Alberta's remoteness from other industrial areas coupled with the demand by the Alberta economy for light engineering commodities act to increase the extent of its inter-industrial linkage beyond that which would occur if major suppliers of these industrial commodities were geographically closer to Alberta. Although the specific nature of Alberta's inter-industry linkages is beyond examination in this report, one cannot help but wonder if most of the Alberta industries supplying the provincial industrial and consumer market do have in common such factors as high friction of distance on their products, or markets in which custom—as distinct from standard—products are demanded.

DISCUSSION

Linkages and Industrial Complexity

What do backward and forward industrial linkages with other Alberta manufacturers reveal about the province's aggregate secondary industrial economy? Approximately one-quarter of Alberta's purchases and shipment of manufactured goods is associated with industries in the province of Alberta; the magnitude of Alberta's inter-industry linkages with the Alberta economy, however, is biased toward forward linkages by a factor of 2.5.:1. Industrial linkages with the provincial economy attest to the province's smaller role as a purchaser of value previously added to Alberta commodities, than as a provider of industrial wealth and utility to itself.

Alberta as a manufacturing system, however, is not entirely dependent on sales within itself. Approximately one-half of the manufactured output leaves the province although it is not possible to specify the extent to which Alberta manufacturers supply extra-provincial manufacturers as distinct from final consumers. Alberta's manufacturing function cannot, therefore, be described as solely satisfying regional consumers. Alberta's manufacturing economy is diverse. Alberta's inter-industry linkages are not uniform; this suggests that some sectors of its manufacturing economy are provincially much less integrated than others. Those industrial groups which assemble diverse processed commodities still rely heavily on extra-provincial purchases and suppliers. Industries not associated with manufacture of food and beverages, or non-metallic mineral products, suggest by the nature of their backward linkages that much of the province's secondary industrial base is related to the assembly and fabrication of products from sub-components supplied by extra-regional suppliers. This heavy reliance on extra-regional suppliers of industrial sub-components and manufactured items in general attests to the relatively small size of the regional population, and to many structural characteristics of the Canadian economy which are frequently cited in explanation of regional economic imbalance in the country.

An important segment of Alberta's manufacturing economy is related to the final stages of various national and international production chains. The province obviously has numerous industrial relations with other urban-industrial places. While not the focus of this particular study, examination of Edmonton's extra-provincial

61

inter-industry linkages would add further to our understanding of the province's manufacturing function. The general effect of friction of distance and extra-regional agglomeration economies on the provincial manufacturing economy is not clear and can only be approached in very loose terms at the moment. Similarly the extent to which general external economies are operating within the province cannot yet be meaningfully specified.

Alberta at the present time has a weakly-developed regional industrial complex. Provincial inter-industry linkages are relatively greater in number than in value. In the assembly and light manufacturing industries, supply ties with extra-regional producers are much stronger than those within the province. For many groups one can probably identify the beginnings, or at least the existence, of a weak industrial complex but one cannot with any confidence, given the great data limitations, yet be sure if the provincial inter-industry linkages of Alberta manufacturers are becoming stronger or weaker, more specific or more diverse. The effect on Alberta's inter-industry manufacturing linkages of decline in exploration and development in the provincial *conventional* petroleum industry concurrent with an increase in these activities in the north can only be surmised. Similarly the effect of change in other industrial regions of the world on Alberta's spatial industrial linkage cannot be clearly identified. These processes, and many others, must, however, be identified and considered before many of the problems facing the Albertan economy can be properly identified and effectively solved.

The present study—one component of a larger work investigating the nature of manufacturing linkages within the Alberta spatial economy, and the perception of locational opportunities and realities by Alberta industrial decision makers—raises far more questions than it answers. The study is based on data for which there are no published equivalents. The data themselves, however, are suggestive rather than definitive because of the variation in the way in which questionnaires were understood and completed by the respondents. Some of the specific observations in this paper may in fact reflect a particular data base rather than the objective structure of Alberta's manufacturing. However, notwithstanding some of these limitations, and despite the relative simplicity of the questionnaire, the nature of Alberta's backward and forward inter-industry provincial linkages has been described and tentatively evaluated. Many additional avenues of enquiry could, and should, be followed from here.

ACKNOWLEDGMENTS

This study was financed by a grant from the Canada Council, and from The University of Calgary Grants Committee. The authors gratefully acknowledge the assistance of Mrs. Eileen Souesmith,

Miss Janet March, and Mr. Patrick Gadden during the long period in which this research was undertaken. The authors are especially indebted to those members of the business community who gave of their time in completing the questionnaire.

REFERENCES

[1] J.N. Britton, "A Geographical Approach to the Examination of Industrial Linkages," *The Canadian Geographer*, 13, No. 3 (1969), 185-198; N.M. Gilmour, "Some Considerations of Spatial Separation between Linked Industries," *The Canadian Geographer*, 15, No. 4, (1971), 287-294; G.J. Karaska, "Manufacturing Linkages in the Philadelphia Economy: Some Evidence of External Agglomeration Forces," 256-267 in L.S. Bourne, (ed.) *Internal Structure of the City*, (New York: Oxford University Press, 1971).

[2] G. Hodge and C.C. Wong, "Adapting Industrial Complex Analysis to the Realities of Regional Data," *Papers, The Regional Science Association*, 28, (1972), 145-166.

[3] G.P.F. Steed, "Changing Linkages and Internal Multiplier of an Industrial Complex," *The Canadian Geographer*, 14, No. 3, (1970), 229-242; "The Northern Ireland Linen Complex, 1950-1970," *Annals, AAG*, 64, No. 3, (1974), 397-408.

[4] W.F. Lever, "Industrial Movement, Spatial Association and Functional Linkages," *Regional Studies*, 6, (1972), 371-384; M.J. Moseley and P.M. Townroe, "Linkage Adjustment Following Industrial Movement," *Tijdschrift voor Econ. en Geografie*, 64, No. 3, (1973), 137-144.

[5] The inter-industry linkages of Edmonton and Calgary are analyzed separately in related studies: B.M. Barr, "The Importance of Regional Inter-Industry Linkages to Calgary's Manufacturing Firms," forthcoming in B.M. Barr, (ed.), *Calgary: Metropolitan Structure and Influence*, (Victoria: University of Victoria, Department of Geography, Western Geographical Series); B.M. Barr and K.J. Fairbairn, "Regional Inter-Industry Linkages in Edmonton's Manufacturing Economy," forthcoming in P.J. Smith, (ed.) *Economic and Urban Analyses of Edmonton*, (Western Geographical Series, The University of Victoria).

[6] Britton, *op. cit.*

[7] Karaska, *op. cit.*

[8] C.E. Richter, "The Impact of Industrial Linkages on Geographic Association," *Journal of Regional Science*, 9, No. 1, (1969), 19-28.

[9] M.E. Streit, "Spatial Associations and Economic Linkages Between Industries," *Journal of Regional Science*, 9, No. 2, (1969), 177-188.

[10] Gilmour, *op. cit.*

[11] S. Czamanski, *Study of Clustering of Industries*, (Halifax: Institute of Public Affairs, Dalhousie University, 1974).

[12] C.G. Schmidt, "Firm Linkage and Structural Change: A Graph Theoretical Analysis," *Economic Geography*, 51, No. 1, (1975), 27-36.

[13] W. Thompson, *A Preface to Urban Economics*, (Baltimore: The Johns Hopkins Press, 1965); "Internal and External Factors in the Development of Urban Economies," 43-62 in H.S. Perloff and L. Wingo, Jr., (eds.), *Issues in Urban Economics*, (Baltimore: Johns Hopkins Press, 1968).

[14] W.B. Beyers, "On Geographical Properties of Growth Center Linkage Systems," *Economic Geography*, 50, No. 3, (1974), 203-218.

[15] J. Campbell, "Selected Aspects of the Interindustry Structure of the State of Washington, 1967," *Economic Geography*, 50, No. 1, (1974), 35-46.

[16] M.J. Moseley, "The Impact of Growth Centres in Rural Regions-I," *Regional Studies*, 7, (1973), 57-75.

[17] W.F. Lever, *op. cit.*

[18] Hodge and Wong, *op. cit.*

[19] Steed, *op. cit.*

[20] Schmidt, *op. cit.*

[21] M.J. Taylor, "Local Linkage, External Economies and the Ironfoundry Industry of the West Midlands and East Lancashire Conurbations," *Regional Studies*, 7, (1973), 387-400.

[22] See the numerous chapters on this subject in F.E.I. Hamilton, *Spatial Perspectives on Industrial Organization and Decision-making*, (London: John Wiley and Sons, 1974).

[23] Schmidt, *op. cit.*, 27.

[24] Thompson, *op. cit.*

[25] *Ibid.*, 46.

[26] Task Force on Urbanization, *Index of Urban and Regional Studies Province of Alberta, 1950-1974*, (Edmonton, 1975).

[27] R.W. Wright, "The Alberta Economy--An Input/Output Analysis," (Report prepared for Calgary Power, 1966, 64 pages).

[28] *Ibid.*, Figure 7.

[29] E.J. Hanson, *Dynamic Decade (The Evolution and Effects of the Oil Industry in Alberta)*, (Toronto: McClelland and Stewart, 1958; "Regional Employment and Income Effects of the Petroleum Industry in Alberta," in *Proceedings of the Council of Economics*, (American Institute of Mining, Metallurgical and Petroleum Engineers, New York, 1966, 38 pages).

[30] S.E. Drugge, "The Location of the Energy Intensive Industries," (Alberta Human Resources Research Council, 1972); "The Attraction of Industry to Alberta," (Alberta Research Council, 1972).

[31] P.J. Smith, "Calgary: A Study in Urban Pattern," *Economic Geography*, 39, No. 4, (1962), 15 pages; "Fort Saskatchewan: An Industrial Satellite of Edmonton," *Plan*, 3, No. 1, (1962), 13 pages.

[32] R. Leigh and D. Carter, "Spatial Pattern of Economic Growth in Alberta, 1961-1966," *The Albertan Geographer*, No. 8, (1972), 7 pages.

[33] N.R. Seifried, "An Analysis of Recent Changes in Manufacturing in Alberta," *The Albertan Geographer*, No. 5, (1969), 6 pages.

[34] B.M. Barr, "Has the Prairie Region Solved its Economic Problems?," *British Columbia Geographical Series*, 16, (1972), 111-121; "Post War Economic Reorganization of the Canadian Prairie Economy," 65-82, in P.J. Smith (ed.), *The Prairie Provinces*, (Toronto: University of Toronto Press, 1972).

[35] G.H. Zieber, "Inter- and Intra-City Location Patterns of Oil Offices for Calgary and Edmonton, 1950-1970," (Unpublished Doctoral Dissertation, University of Alberta, 1971).

[36] P.J. Curtis, "Some Aspects of Industrial Linkages in Edmonton's Oil Industry: With Special Reference to the Tertiary Sector," (Unpublished Master's Thesis, University of Alberta, 1972).

[37] L.S. Wilson, "Some Factors Relating to the Attraction of Manufacturing Industries to the Province of Alberta," (Unpublished Master's Thesis, University of Alberta, 1971).

THE SOUTH SHORE OF BURRARD INLET, VANCOUVER, B. C. --
A LANDUSE CONFLICT OVER AN OIL REFINERY EXPANSION

J. H. Bradbury
Simon Fraser University

INTRODUCTION

The ownership of land has had numerous different meanings through time and within different cultures. Land has been variously seen, for example, as the source of joy and life for some peasant cultures, or as the symbol of power and status for others. The Australian Aborginals'[1] conception of land tenure is, needless to say, quite different from the meaning of land ownership developed in many post-industrial societies, wherein land is an essential item of investment and trade in a property market-arena.[2]

A basic tenet of land ownership in a capitalistic system is the notion of the inalienable right of institutions and individuals to put land to the use which best fits the interests of the primary party, the landowner. Except where any landuse runs contrary to special by-laws and various levels of governmental jurisdiction, this assumption of the right to use land in the best interests of the owner has been the usual method of assigning land uses both within cities and in rural farming landscapes. One consequence of this form of land ownership is a conflict over landuse which may arise from the opposing precepts of different interest groups.[3]

Form has suggested that the "image of a free and unorganized market in which individuals compete impersonally for land must be abandoned. The reason for this is that the land market is highly organized and dominated by a number of interacting organizations."[4] According to Form, four types of social congeries dominate the land market and determine the use of land: (1) real estate and developer groups including the construction industry, (2) larger industries, businesses and utilities, (3) individual house owners and other small consumers of land, and (4) local governmental agencies.[5] Many models of landuse conflict show the parties involved as equal competitors for the right firstly to own land, and secondly to use it in a manner befitting their requirements. Form's model, for instance, enables the identification of the power groups involved but makes no assessment of the difference in influence of each.

In recent years conflicts have increased among the groups represented in Form's model: the developers, industry, houseowners and local government. The most widely known and one of the earliest is the Boston Common conflict portrayed by Walter Firey;[6] others that come readily to mind are the Spadina freeway in Toronto[7] or the Strathcona project in Vancouver. Three features emerge from these conflicts. First, that competition was seldom equal because invariably some competitors were better armed than others. Secondly, particularly in conflicts between industry or local government and citizens and neighbourhoods, citizens have been increasingly vociferous in their demands for more control over landuse. Thirdly, a polarization of values and attitudes has become increasingly evident, and in many cases emotional. Industrial development has become totally unacceptable or all good. Pollution, whether of water or air is acceptable as a trade-off for other benefits, or is rejected because of its adverse or noxious effects. Industry adjacent to housing may become acceptable because industry represents jobs; or the intrusion of industry into living space may be seen as undesirable because of its impact on property values, or because of its deleterious effects on the liveability of the area.

Landuse conflicts within cities and in urban fringe zones have also been analyzed purely as competition for land as a scarce commodity.[8] Urban theory linked to such landuse conflict has taken the view that the competition takes place in a property market-arena in which the combatants thrust and parry over a land costing mechanism, namely the real property market, which determines the price and the use of a particular plot of land. However, a competition model does not accommodate the numerous related facets which evolve in complex landuse conflicts--for instance, urban renewal, industrial expansion or freeway extensions in city centres. A competition model conceals the intricacies and complexities of community, corporate, and government involvement in landuse conflicts occurring between unequal parties often involving jurisdictional questions between two or more levels of government.

This paper examines the expansion of an oil refinery in Greater Vancouver, British Columbia. Such heavy industrial landuse within an urban area raises further questions which cannot be dealt with by models which assume either equal competition between parties or competition over land as a scarce commodity as basic. For instance, questions related to the role of public policy and public demand for the commodity need to be accommodated. Other pertinent

considerations are the scale of an industrial plant within the urban
area, the impact of a facility on existing items of the urban landscape, and the degree of toxicity or perceived noxiousness of a
facility.

Conflict over land then, occurs not only over who shall use
it, but also over the use to which it shall be put. The competition
is seldom equal, and is often not purely economic. There are conflicts of values between involved groups and differences in their
power bases. Citizen groups are increasingly refusing to be de-
terred by their evident weakness as a pressure group, and as a result more and more controversy is arising over the perceived inalienable right of any company or individual to use land purely as
it wishes.

Examination of the conflict which arose over the proposed
expansion of an oil refinery on the south shore of Burrard Inlet in
Vancouver, British Columbia provides a case study which helps to
identify both the unequal competition between interested bodies and
the many factors involved in any one landuse conflict.

THE SOUTH SHORE OF BURRARD INLET: THE OIL REFINERY

Proposals to expand an oil refinery within a suburban area
adjacent to Eastern Burrard Inlet in Vancouver, British Columbia,
led between 1973 and 1975 to a landuse conflict involving the
Chevron Oil Company, the surrounding neighbourhoods, the Municipal
Corporation, and the British Columbia Provincial government. The
conflict was not limited to competition for land as a scarce resource. Indeed, the Company was requesting permission to expand its
refining capacity within its existing boundaries.[9] Rather, the
conflict arose from opposition to continued industrial landuse next
to living spaces, from an increased awareness of the implications
of noxious industry proximate to living space, and from an awareness
of the competition for other landuse priorities in urban areas.

The situation arose originally in 1971 when the Chevron Oil
Company proposed an expansion of its refinery on the south shore of
Burrard Inlet. It concluded in 1975 when the British Columbia
Provincial government finally gave permission for an expansion to
proceed. The intervening period of five years of protracted decision
making demonstrated quite clearly the broad spectrum of corporate and
community interactions surrounding a landuse conflict of this nature.

The presence of oil refineries and other heavy industrial
plants on the south shore of the Burrard Inlet in Burnaby dates from
1932 (a Shell Oil plant) and from March, 1935, when the Standard Oil
Company purchased 45 acres of land for a refinery for $12,500. Fig-
ure 1 illustrates the density of housing and the relationship of the
oil Refinery site to this housing in 1935 when the land was purchased

69

Fig.(1)

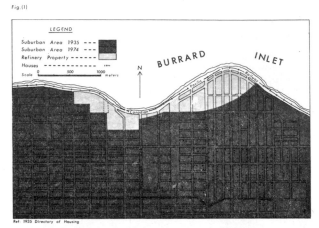

North Burnaby Suburban Fringe Area --- 1935&1974

by the Standard Chevron company.[10]   In 1935 the area of Burnaby shown
in Figure I was a working class suburban dormitory adjacent to the
city of Vancouver. Burnaby had been forced into receivership by a
government-appointed commissioner in 1932 because of the impact of
the 1930's. Depression-weary ratepayers, welcoming the chance of a
new industry which would provide jobs and increase the tax base,
were in no position to complain that the oil refinery would be close
to their houses.[11]

        In 1935 the area immediately surrounding the oil refinery
was the most densely populated in the suburb of Burnaby (Figure I).
Over the years the refinery expanded its boundaries, buying up land
and houses on its periphery. In 1974 it owned 31 houses on the
perimeter of the refinery.[12] Householders on the perimeter had on
occasion been moved from house to house as the refinery expanded between 1935 and 1974. Even though conflict between the refinery landuse and residential landuse had occurred on several occasions between 1935 and 1974, the proposed expansion in 1974 sparked the most
controversy.

        The Chevron Oil Company in 1974 submitted to the Burnaby
Municipal Council a further proposal to expand the refinery. The
Company had wanted to expand in 1971 but their request had been
tabled by the Council. The "oil crisis" provided a rationale for

the Company to re-activate the application. The market demand in British Columbia for refined oil products in 1974 and 1975, together with an apparent "oil crisis" in 1974 provided some support for plans to renew and expand the plant. Demand in 1974 for refined oil was approximately 160,000 bpd; of this amount the province's refineries produced 136,000 bpd, leaving a shortfall of 24,000 bpd. The Chevron expansion was expected to cover some of this shortfall.[13] The plans for expansion of the refinery capacity involved the renewal of a large portion of the plant in order to comply with regulations regarding the expulsion of both gaseous and liquid effluent,[14] and the installation of plant equipment to reduce the amount of sulphur dioxide in the atmosphere--a matter which had been contentious for some years in the surrounding community of Burnaby. The pollution control laws of British Columbia, which were under revision (and under question) during 1974, required that significant reductions be made in levels of nitrogen oxides and hydrocarbons expelled into the atmosphere. In effect, expansion of the refinery had to involve improvements, for only if the plant remained unchanged could the pollution level remain as high as it was. The expansion plans thus involved the renewal of the "offending" sections of the refinery to reduce levels of pollution.

The Chevron refinery involved is one of four located on Burrard Inlet in the Greater Vancouver area. The question of expansion of one refinery raised the possibility of a "domino-expansion" of other refining units on the Inlet.[15] Thus the landuse conflict arising from one case was a possible forerunner of other conflicts. The circumstances of energy demand in that year precipitated and highlighted the whole landuse conflict. With little possibility of expansion on an alternative site without very expensive relocation costs the problems of the energy demand and landuse conflict became closely intermeshed, with community and industrial exponents clearly split on the matter.

THE MUNICIPAL GOVERNMENT RESPONSE

The Chevron Oil Company on April 13, 1971, made its first approaches to the Burnaby Municipal Council to modernize and expand. The Council was split on the matter but on July 12, 1971, it approved the modernization plans, while at the same time stating that the action did not constitute tacit approval of future expansion of any refinery within the municipality. The Council resolved also to proceed with an investigation of ways and means of limiting or confining any future expansion of the productive facilities of all other Burnaby refineries. On November 15, 1971 the Council revoked this latter resolution and decided to proceed with an investigation of ways and means to set standards for aesthetic or visual pollution and control, and for the level and quality of emissions from the refineries, as well as possible enforcement procedures.

71

In 1973 the Oil Company again asked for permission to expand its refining capacity. The request arrived at Municipal Hall on June 11, addressed to Council members. A by-election was held on June 13, in which there was little mention of the refinery expansion. The Chevron Company brief of June 11, however, arrived on council members' desks eight days after the November 17 regular municipal elections--prior to which no mention of refinery expansion had been made--and six months after it had been received.[16] No clear reason was given for this delay although speculation did occur. Finally, in January 1974, a public meeting was held between interested citizens, the oil company and the municipality.[17] At that meeting the Municipal Council gave its permission for the expansion to proceed.

THE COMMUNITY RESPONSE

Debate about the proposed expansion fluctuated within the community of North Burnaby. Some saw it as an undesirable and unnecessary expansion of heavy industry within a valued suburban living space. Others saw it as a welcome addition to the local employment situation and to the municipal tax base. Many considered it hopeless to oppose a corporation as large as the Chevron Standard Oil Company. Others argued against the continued presence of industry next to housing, against the industrial use of waterfront land and against the possible combined pollution from the oil refinery. Between 1973 and 1975 a community protest group was formed which mounted several appeals to the Oil Company, to the Council, the regional government, and finally to the Provincial government in Victoria.[18]

The release of the expansion plans in late 1973 suggested to residents of the local area that a threat existed. The increase in plant capacity and possible additional air pollution suggested to them a further undesirable intrusion of heavy industry was about to occur in the neighbourhood. The perceived threat led to a sense of solidarity that had previously been absent in the sporadic attempts to oppose the presence of the refinery next to their housing. Lotz (1970) has suggested that in conditions such as these people communicate their fears to others, and a sense of unity begins to grow in the face of what is seen to be a common threat.[19]

A group of residents living within 2 to 4 km. of the refinery, and numbering between 900 and 1,000 individuals, saw the expansion as a threat to their life style; a life style which embraced land and home ownership on small, individual urban lots.[20] Secondly, the residents recognized a sense of place or belonging in the area which was expressed in parochial and sentimental attachment to houses and neighbourhoods. The latter was reinforced by reference to the equity of properties owned by the residents. The fear that property values would be lowered by the expansion of a noxious industry was also expressed on numerous occasions by these same people. Both Lotz and

72

Harvey indicate that similar responses have been noted in other communities faced with highway clearances, real estate speculation, public utility expansion or the expansion of noxious industries.[21]

People living around the refinery had been aware for many years of its existence as a noxious facility and as a blight and depressant on housing quality and values. But it was the act of proposing a new expansion which first of all precipitated a response from the citizens who were most sensitive to the physical, environmental and aesthetic impact of heavy industry on their living spaces. This elicited a small core of activists who focussed their activities on petitions, briefs to various levels of government, political lobbying at various levels, public meetings, and presentations to the media for publicity purposes. A second level of response came from the residents who actually signed the petitions and who listened to media commentaries, but who never became actively involved in protest. It was only when a threat to destroy houses for a buffer zone (Figure II) was made in late 1974 that this second group became active[22]—they were a ratepayers group in existence for some 20 years that had actively opposed the refinery on previous occasions.

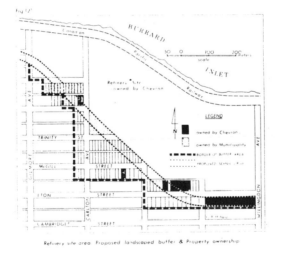

Refinery site area. Proposed landscaped buffer & Property ownership.

The voting patterns in the 1974 municipal election for councillors in the municipality indicate the degree of opposition to expansion of the oil refinery. Two opposing party platforms in that election presented different views on the expansion proposal. The

73

party which opposed expansion received 23% of its support in the four polling areas surrounding the refinery, while the party supporting refinery expansion received only 12% of its votes from that area.[23] At the public meeting conducted by the Municipal Council in January 1974 at which the issue of the refinery expansion was first publicly discussed, 650 of the 800 persons present opposed the scheme. Neither these figures or the voting results from the 1974 election in the polling divisions adjacent to the refinery, however, give an accurate picture of the extent to which the refinery expansion was opposed or approved within Burnaby. In the 1974 election, voters who lived in close proximity to the refinery voted for candidates who campaigned against the expansion whereas voters in the rest of Burnaby voted for candidates who supported expansion. However because it was not possible to ascertain these particular divisions on the basis of issues which became apparent during the election campaign we can only strongly suggest that the division between voters who were near or distant

Fig. (3)

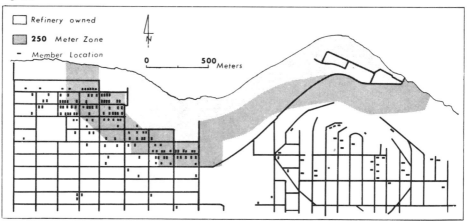

Citizens Group Member Location **1974**

were indeed due to the refinery expansion issue. If we accept this conclusion, then we can surmise that the perception of the refinery expansion as a threat was localized to a ring around the refinery. This conclusion concurs with other findings on local issues in neighbourhood areas. These findings suggest that, except where issues appear to be of considerable importance to a wide group of persons dispersed over a wide area, the effect of the issue will be largely insular and confined to those individuals who consider themselves to be most affected or most likely to be affected.

Figure III shows the areal extent of the perceived threat of the expansion and buffer zone program. The threat is measured here by the location of the members of a citizens' group which voiced opposition to the expansion plans. Although the greater proportion of the response to the threat came from close by the refinery perimeter, a significant group up to 0.5-1.0 km. distance also saw expansion as undesirable. A second citizens' association, not recorded on this map, also voiced opposition to industrial expansion, but only became active when a physical threat to housing was applied under a buffer zone plan (Figure II). Many citizens responded in a manner which could be classified as a protest only after the ultimate threat to houses and owner-occupied land became evident in the area surrounding the refinery.

THE BUFFER ZONE PLAN

The plan for creating a buffer zone around the refinery was first revealed after the 1974 municipal election. Under this plan (Figure II) approximately 100 houses were to be demolished for a green space between the industry and housing.

Property purchases by the Chevron Oil Company within the buffer zone, but outside the refinery boundary line,[24] preceded publication of the plan. The purchases were interpreted by some residents as a premature expansion of the company's activities, and by others as a block-busting technique to enable the Company to consolidate its tenure quickly and cheaply, preparatory to further property purchase and expansion.

The extent of the planned buffer zone between industrial landuse and residential landuse was clear. The notation "Proposed Scenic Drive" indicates the boundaries between oil refinery land, municipal land and residential areas. The refinery land was zoned for industrial use, while portions of the municipal land were zoned for parks and a buffer area. All other land was zoned residential, but within that area, lots and houses were owned by the oil company and were used in 1974 as part of a land exchange with the municipality to enable the company to consolidate its holdings and more firmly to establish boundary lines. The notation, "Border of buffer area," indicating the east-west line of demarcation within the residential zone is associated with a proposed buffer zone extending inland from the Coast. Between the eastern and western boundaries all houses marked as city lots on Figure II were scheduled for demolition. The Municipal Council and the Municipal Planning Department were in favour of the buffer zone because they believed that housing should be separated from industry. However residents within 200 metres of the refinery were opposed because it meant the destruction of houses.

CONCLUSION

Three main groups were involved in the conflict over the Chevron expansion. The Company requested expansion, council eventually supported it, and a citizen group, the Burnaby Concerned Citizens, opposed it. The citizen group fluctuated in its level of activity and its methods. Letters were written to Council and other levels of government, and signatures were collected on petitions and presented to the municipal council and the provincial government. Appeals were launched to the municipal council, the regional government (Greater Vancouver Regional District), the provincial Pollution Control Board, and the provincial government Cabinet. A small core of people were involved with community organizations, and a wider group were involved with public meetings and a street demonstration.

The citizen group did not win its case. The oil company was in a powerful bargaining position; oil was needed, and relocation of the existing plant would probably have been beyond the financial ability of the Burnaby municipality.[25] Members of the municipal council opposed to the expansion were in the minority. The other councillors chose to treat citizen opposition as a very localized issue which they could safely vote against. The citizen group itself never gathered enough support or publicity to change this attitude.

Once the council had accepted the idea of expansion, members of the community proximate to the refinery were reluctant to place much faith in the success of appeals. Only the question of the buffer zone again aroused community involvement--but the very debating of that as an issue was an implicit acceptance of the fact that the expansion was a *fait accompli*.

This conflict was over land as a scarce commodity, not solely in terms of its price in a property market arena, but more in respect of its limited availability in a specific area of Greater Vancouver. Residents in the suburban area of North Burnaby felt that priorities should have been assigned to land uses in the Lower Mainland area of British Columbia--oil refineries should be located elsewhere than the shores of Burrard Inlet within the city boundaries. The major issue was the use to which the land should be put. Some citizens would not accept that the oil company had a right to use the land as it wished even though that land had belonged to the company for forty years. The company naturally believed it had that right as long as it complied with pollution regulations and was a "good corporate citizen" and a "good neighbour." The competition in the conflict was certainly not equal; most large corporations whose interests are at stake can draw on financial and legal expertise and resources which generally far exceed those of a community group.

SOURCES

[1] See also discussion of land ownership in Stewart L. Udall, *The Quiet Crisis* (New York: Holt, Rinehart and Winston Ind., 1963). The book includes a discussion on land wisdom and perceptions of land tenure of North American Indians.

[2] W. Alsonso, *Location and Landuse: Toward a General Theory of Land Rent* (Cambridge, Mass.: Harvard University Press, 1964). See also D.A. Muncy, "Land for industry--a neglected problem," in H.M. Mayer and C.F. Kohn (eds.), *Readings in Urban Geography* (Chicago: The University of Chicago Press, 1959), 464-77. (Originally published in *Harvard Business Review*, XXXII, March-April, 1954).

[3] R.T. Ernst, L. Hugg & R.A. Crooker. "Competition and Conflict over Landuse Change in the Inner-City: Institution Versus Community," *Antipode*, 6, (1974), 70-97.

[4] William H. Form, "The place of the Social Structure in the determination of land use: some implications for a theory of urban ecology," *Social Forces*, 32, (May, 1954), 317.

[5] Form, *op. cit.*, 318.

[6] Walter Firey, *Land use in Central Boston* (Cambridge: Harvard University Press, 1946).

[7] See discussions on Spadina Freeway in R.R. Krueger and R.C. Bryfogle (eds.), *Urban Problems: a Canadian Reader* (Toronto: Holt, Rinehart and Winston of Canada, 1971), 204-214. See also D. & N. Nowlan, *The Bad Trip: the Untold Story of the Spadina Expressway* (Toronto: New Press, 1970).

[8] Ernst, *op. cit.*

[9] Chevron Canada Limited, *Expansion Proposal Burnaby Refinery*, June 11, 1973. A proposal to Burnaby Municipal Council, June, 1973.

[10] *British Columbia Directory, 1935* (Vancouver, B.C.: Wrigleys Publishing Company, 1935).

[11] B. Bradbury, *The Road to Receivership: Unemployment and Relief in Burnaby, North Vancouver City and District and West Vancouver, 1929-1933* (unpublished M.A. thesis, Simon Fraser University, 1975).

[12] Burnaby Municipal Council. Item 18. Manager's Report, #11, November 18, 1974. "Proposed Highway Exchange and Land Exchange--Chevron Site--attachment #2"; item 18, Manager's Report #11. February 17, 1975. "Chevron Properties and houses--apparent conditions of houses--page 162, Attachment #2."

[13] British Columbia Energy Commission--correspondence. Item 10. Manager's Report #3, January 14, 1974, "Proposed Chevron Refinery Expansion," and B.M. Gunn, "British Columbia Refinery Expansion and Long Term Policy of Refinery Location," an unpublished brief presented to British Columbia Petroleum Corporation, June 14, 1974, 2-3.

[14] Chevron Canada Ltd., *op. cit.*

[15] Gunn, *op. cit.*

[16] Burnaby Municipal Council. Item 29. Manager's Report #88, November 26, 1973, "Proposed Chevron Refinery Expansion Program Master Plan and Burnaby Municipal Council"; item 31. Manager's Report #92, December 10, 1973, "Proposed Chevron Refinery Expansion Program."

[17] Burnaby Municipal Council. Item 10. Manager's Report #3, January 14, 1974, "Proposed Chevron Refinery Expansion."

[18] Burnaby Concerned Citizens Association, unpublished brief to Greater Vancouver Regional District Planning Committee--17th April, 1974; Gunn, *op. cit.*; and North Slope Ratepayers Association, an unpublished brief presented to Burnaby Municipal Council, February 28, 1975, 2.

[19] J.R. Lotz, "Citizens Participation," *Habitat,* 13, (1970), 17.

[20] The figure of 900 to 1,000 persons is derived from various petition lists circulated in the district within 2 to 4 km. of the refinery. It is not possible to estimate the total number involved in the conflict at any one time. The only other indication of numbers involved comes from the attendance at a public meeting on January 14, 1974--approximately 800 persons were present.

[21] Lotz, *op. cit.*; David Harvey, *Society, the City and the Space-Economy of Urbanism*, Commission on College Geography, Resource Paper No. 18 (Washington, D.C.: Association of American Geographers, 1973), 11.

[22] Northslope Ratepayers Association, 1975, *op. cit.*

[23] Municipal election results by polling place, Burnaby, B.C. Municipal elections, 1974.

[24] Burnaby Municipal Council. Item 18. Manager's Report #11, February 17, 1975. "Chevron Canada Limited: Project Implementation," 133-167.

[25] J.H. Bradbury, "Oil Refineries on the Burrard Inlet," *Proceedings of Vancouver Waterfront Conference,* May 3-4, 1974, 49-51.

POINT ROBERTS AND THE INTERNATIONAL JOINT COMMISSION
UNITED STATES AND CANADA[1]

Manfred C. Vernon
Western Washington State College

On April 21, 1971 the Governments of the United States and
Canada, pursuant to Article IX of the Boundary Waters Treaty of January 11, 1909, requested the International Joint Commission United
States and Canada (IJC) "to investigate and recommend measures to
alleviate certain conditions of life of residents of Point Roberts,
in the State of Washington." Some of these problems "created or
magnified by the presence and location of the international boundary
at Point Roberts" were described as pertaining to the application of
customs laws and regulations as well as those dealing with employment
of Point Roberts residents, or of Canadian citizens resident in Point
Roberts, in Canada.[2]

Other problems dealt with health and medical services, the
existing arrangements for the supply of electric power and telephone
services, and the matter of law enforcement, in particular the
question of transporting accused persons from Point Roberts to detention facilities in the United States by way of Canada. Finally,
the request included also a general suggestion to make a study of
"any other problems found to exist on account of the unique situation
of Point Roberts."[3]

Point Roberts consists of about five square miles of land
located below the forty-ninth parallel at the southern extremity of
the peninsula which projects south from Vancouver, British Columbia
and separates the Strait of Georgia from Boundary Bay. The request
of the two governments referred to a permanently residing population
of approximately 300 persons, "although the summer population, due
to recreational advantages of the Point, is approximately 3,500."
Most of the land owners in Point Roberts are Canadian (upward of 80
per cent) while most of the land is owned by Americans. There have
been major efforts to make much of the land available to a developing

firm in order to develop a recreation-retirement community. While
there exists no physical connection to any point within the United
States it is, because of its location below the forty-ninth parallel,
territory of the United States and thus an American exclave. For
some time prior to the request, the people of Point Roberts had
asked for assistance in solving problems that were the result of the
"isolation" from the United States for reasons of the international
boundary.[4] In fact, the Point can only be reached overland by a
person coming from the United States crossing the Canadian border at
Blaine, Washington, and traveling through Canada for about 25 miles
before finally passing through the United States border station at
Point Roberts. A few years before the request to the IJC, a Memorial
had been introduced in the Washington State Senate on February 19,
1969, urging the Congress of the United States to take whatever
action would be necessary to hold a joint conference with the appropriate representatives of Canada in order to discuss the problems of
Point Roberts.[5]

Subsequently, in pursuance to the Reference of April 21, 1971,
the IJC established the International Point Roberts Board on November
30, 1971,

> to undertake, through appropriate agencies and departments in
> Canada and the United States the necessary investigations and
> studies and to advise the Commission on all matters which it
> must consider in making a report or reports under the said
> Reference.[6]

In addition to this general instruction, the *Directive* included all
points of concern that had been mentioned in the correspondence of
the two governments to the IJC; it also asked advice with reference
to "any other problems found to exist on account of the unique situation of Point Roberts."

The Board was requested to do its work and carry out the program in accordance with the outline approved by the Commission, meaning
that any modification or change could be undertaken only with the
Commission's approval. It was also instructed neither to conduct
public hearings nor to make public any of its proceedings or under-
takings until released by the Commission.

The membership of the Board was to consist of a United States
Section and a Canadian Section, each with three members. The members
of the Board were officially introduced by the Commission on the
occasion of a public hearing at Point Roberts on December 18, 1971.[7]
The Board met thereafter on numerous occasions; its final *Report* was
submitted to the IJC in October, 1973.

Interestingly enough, the outstanding problem for Point Roberts
was one not specifically mentioned in the *Directive* to the Board. The

Board became very soon aware that limited water resources and the lack of adequate sewage treatment facilities would engage its time more than anything else. It was a matter of overpowering concern, particularly since it was noted that "every fine weekend in summer, a Canadian tourist influx of between ten and twenty thousand persons . . . put additional pressure on the Point's resources."[8] It was also observed that, at times, the water shortage proved to be critical just for the existing population. Thus one feared that without sufficient water in supply, the residents of Point Roberts would lack basic services taken for granted by most communities in the United States. It became clear that the proximity of sufficient water supply in British Columbia could be of no help because of a Canadian policy concept not to make water available for exportation. On the occasion of the Public Hearings on its *Report* in December 1973, both the Canadian and the United States Chairmen summed up the Board's findings as follows:

> The most logical source of the basic services is from the vast resources of British Columbia. To date, however, the Government of British Columbia has been unwilling to provide them to the Point although they have stated that water would be provided in the event of extreme emergency such as for the purpose of fire protection.

Altogether, no major understanding was reached in regard to most of the controversial points. Certainly, the water question resulted in an impasse. On the other hand, some conditions were improved, as in the case of Canadian physicians being permitted to practice medicine at Point Roberts, at least to a limited degree, viz., to respond to emergencies and make house calls, but not to open offices at the Point.[9]

Under these circumstances the Board decided to give thought to a variety of ideas that might be beneficial to Point Roberts as *long-range* solutions, particularly in regard to water availability which, hopefully would come from Canada after all. One possibility was to "sell, or lease the area to Canada, or otherwise effect a transfer of territory with Canada." But this idea was rejected by the United States section as politically unacceptable to it, just as the possible cession of a strip of Canadian land along Boundary Bay to the United States for a road of access to the Point was not deemed politically feasible to the Canadian Board members. Any transfer of territorial sovereignty was thus out of the question.[10]

The Board therefore looked into other possible long-range solutions possibly helpful to Point Roberts and its people. These were:

1. Private development of Point Roberts to accommodate a sufficient increase in the population of Point Roberts to justify

the provision of normal public service there, e.g., adequate water
supply and waste disposal system, fire and police protection, school
facilities, etc.;

  2. The establishment of a Washington State Park at Point
Roberts; and

  3. The creation of an "international park" system astride
the border, of which Point Roberts would be a part, and to be pre-
ferably considered as a "conservation and recreation" area.[11]

  It was the considered opinion of the Board that private development of Point Roberts would involve a substantial increase in
the permanent population, and could take place only if water were to
come from the United States mainland; but even then it would probably
become obvious that the Canadian authorities--regional, provincial,
and federal--would deplore the additional burden of an increasing
population on Canadian public facilities, roads, and services. But,
on the other hand, the members of the Board also recognized that if
a developed would supply the

> financing and meet the requirements of the State of Washington,
> private development could come to pass without international
> consultation and cooperation. That is to say that Point Roberts
> is entitled to seek solutions to its own problems, as it sees
> them, if it can obtain adequate financial assistance from the
> government of the State of Washington, and from the United
> States government--or from a private developer with the basic
> means to provide the services required.[12]

  It must be understood that the bi-national Board was most
sensitive to the international aspects of the total problem. While
the predominant point of view on the part of the United States was
one to favour the transfer of territory, the main Canadian concern
was one of opposition to a substantial population increase at the
Point, since this would have a considerable impact on the roads of
access to the Point, and would lead to a significant increase in the
workload of the small Canadian customs station at that border. Thus,
the Board gave thought to the possibility of finding solutions on
the state--provincial--or national levels but also of developing a
truly international arrangement in the form of a supranational recreation and conservation area. It became clear to the Board that
a park arrangement either under the control of the State of Washington or of the United States, could not be seriously considered;
indeed, it was noted that, from a strictly American point of view,
either solution would be extraordinarily expensive, particularly
were one to think of the rather small number of United States citizens that such a park might ultimately serve. It was also realized
that a park system limited to the area of Point Roberts proper, with
its 3,151 acres, could easily attract great numbers of transient

visitors (likely to be Canadian citizens) and thus "exchange the present problem of residence use and water storage for a problem of recreational users."[13]

Under these circumstances, major consideration was given to the possibility that Point Roberts could become part of an international park system with demonstrable benefits to both the United States and Canada, and "the necessary resources . . . potentially to come from both countries." The Board, with the approval of the IJC, called upon the National Park Services of Canada and of the United States to develop conceptual studies exploring whether Point Roberts could be the focal point of a parks system on both sides of the border "which would offer environmental, recreational, and long-term development advantages attractive to both countries." This resulted in a joint report of both park services, "An Inventory of International Park Possibilities: Point Roberts, Boundary Bay, San Juan and Gulf Islands Archipelago." Several possibilities were envisaged:

A. (1) Point Roberts alone,

    (2) Point Roberts and/or Tsawwassen and Boundary Centennial Beaches,

    (3) Point Roberts, the adjacent beaches, Boundary Bay, and Semiahmoo Bay, or

B. Point Roberts, its environs, and the island archipelago.[14]

The Point Roberts Board, upon studying these proposals, expressed its preference for Concept B as the most desirable solution and to be "most accurately . . . described as a conservation and recreation area." It would stretch from Gabriola Island to Whidbey Island in the San Juan–Gulf Island Archipelago, and from Vancouver Island to the mainland coast of the State of Washington in east-western direction. All told, it would include approximately 3,000 square miles, with more than half of the area being water. Within it would be also all the existing public parks (some 90 of them) as well as fifteen existing bird sanctuaries and wildlife refuges.[15]

The major objective of this international concept would be to preserve the existing attractive characteristics of the island archipelago region astride the border including the preservation of marine and land-based wildlife, archaeological and historic resources, and the maintenance of water quality standards.

In brief, the most salient objective of Concept B is the conservation and preservation of the present characteristics of the San Juan–Gulf Island Archipelago while this is still economically, technologically, and politically feasible.[16]

83

Point Roberts itself, "and an equivalent contiguous area in Canada along the shore of Boundary Bay," would be the headquarters area and, within its confines, there would be a special administrative headquarters sector. A bi-national forum of three Americans and three Canadians with experience and professional knowledge of environmental matters or land use management, or both, would control the conservation area and operate in the headquarters area according to limits defined by the Governments of the United States and Canada. Its primary duty would be "to develop and make policy recommendations for the consideration of" the appropriate Canadian and American authorities. This organization, "perhaps adapted from the model of Campobello International Park, should be analogous to those of the International Joint Commission, i.e., they should be recommendatory in nature insofar as agreed bi-national policy considerations" were concerned. Thus, while the forum would recommend standards to be applied on both sides of the border with respect to water quality, resource conservation, possible land acquisition, population density, recreational facilities and other matters, it was, however, not to interfere with any sovereign expression of either country.[17]

The Point Roberts Board felt that the adoption of its recommendation would considerably alleviate the problems for Point Roberts, yet at the same time preserve the natural beauty of one of the finest recreation areas in the world. It would "provide farsighted protection of the environment in a part of North America that is most worthy of protection and is in foreseeable danger of environmental degradation."[18] It was also assumed that the adoption of Concept B by both countries would lead to the availability of adequate water supplies from British Columbia as "the logical source of water for Point Roberts."

It was to be understood that existing legal arrangements on both sides of the border would remain intact and county and municipal authorities be essentially undisturbed throughout the area. There would be no change in fishing rights, since they were governed by existing treaties and other international agreements.

The public hearings of December 4-8, 1973 on the *Report* were attended by thousands of people and heavily covered by the news media in both countries. The public reaction ranged from voices of total rejection to those of support of the concept. It should be most fairly described as running heavily in opposition to the Board's recommendations. Much of this reaction was probably based on a general misunderstanding of the *Report*, which was only advisory--at best an idea--and conceptual in nature. The many in opposition to it seemingly felt that it had the quality of a binding decision, was largely concerned with the threat of expropriation of individual property, represented the loss of national sovereignty as an international body, or caused danger to specific interests such as fishing.[19]

Subsequently the IJC concluded that there was need for greater specificity and precise definition of the Board's recommendations. Thus the Commission requested the Board, or its individual members, to be available for consultations, on an informal basis, with officials of the various jurisdictions within the total area, and to explain the recommendations in detail. Task forces were to be composed of personnel from the State of Washington and the Province of British Columbia to concern themselves with the feasibility of the general concepts of the plan. Nothing came of the formation of such task forces. Instead, in the case of British Columbia, an Island Trust for the Gulf Island region was developed, while in the State of Washington a number of hearings and meetings were arranged by legislators to talk matters over with local officials and the general public. Finally, the IJC, upon the recommendation of the Board, issued a supplemental report on the occasion of its meeting in Ottawa in October, 1974.[20]

The Board observed that the problems initially identified by the two governments were minor when compared to a number of others more fundamental facing the population of the Point, such as the lack of water to support this population. Since this resource "must come from outside the Point" and the logical place is from Canada, the judgment of the Board was that the Canadian Governments involved will agree to supply water only if they also have a voice in the questions of land use patterns and population densities on Point Roberts.

In its conclusion the Board firmly stated that the "only realistic long-term solutions of the problems facing the residents of Point Roberts will necessarily involve cooperative action by both United States and Canadian authorities." Yet it seemed also apparent to the Board that many other interested parties did not share this conviction and would prefer a local solution.[21]

The study of the total Point Roberts problem has been, since its inception, a concern of other groups and governmental authorities. If it will transpire, as the Board believes it will, that the cooperation of Canadian authorities is indeed required with regard to road access to Point Roberts, to customs and immigration services, or water for both domestic and sanitary purposes, and possibly garbage disposal and other functions, the Board prefers that such cooperation start at the State-Provincial level. In recommending this, the Board also most firmly stated as its considered opinion

> that the job it was given cannot be carried further until the various local and regional authorities agree that bi-national cooperation is required. At that time the IJC may wish to have the comments of the Board on the findings and conclusions of the local officials.

The Board is aware that the Commission may wish in the near

future to make a report to the Point Roberts Reference. Because of the opposition to Concept B expressed at a number of public hearings in the area, the Board doubts that it would now be useful for the Commission to recommend its acceptance by the two Federal Governments. It is also the Board's view that the Board should make no further substantive recommendations regarding Point Roberts unless and until the authorities of the State of Washington and the Province of British Columbia conclude that cooperation on the part of the two Federal Governments is required.[22]

In the meantime, on January 8, 1974, some Senators of the State of Washington introduced a Senate Joint Memorial "respectfully asking that the International Joint Commission discontinue its study of the future of Point Roberts until the authorized county and state agencies complete the land use plan and actions now in process and the Washington State Legislature submits any recommendations that may then be deemed appropriate."

The State Legislature then requested the formation of a Select Committee to "develop suggested policies which would be in the best interests of the State of Washington relating to the future of the Point Roberts area." This Committee held a series of public hearings at Point Roberts, Bellingham, and Friday Harbor in July, 1974. These meetings clearly showed the opposition of most of those in attendance to Concept B, favouring instead local solutions.[23]

In its final report to the 44th Legislature of the State of Washington, the Select Committee expressed its feeling that the major problem facing Point Roberts at the present time is a lack of information concerning potential water sources. Particularly it was felt that it would be essential to ascertain whether there would be an adequate supply of ground water available on Point Roberts, but also whether or not there would be adequate water in the Blaine and Birch Bay areas to serve not only their future needs but still transfer water to the Point if necessary. The Committee's Report of January 13, 1975 concluded with the recommendation that the International Point Roberts Board be disbanded and the problems of Point Roberts be handled on a local basis. It also proposed that its report be presented to the Legislature and the Committee itself be dissolved.[24]

Thus, by now, when a Board and a Select Committee have become silent, the query might very well be: "Is this where all of us came in, or will there be another round on Point Roberts, Washington, in the continuing dialogue of two nations—children of one mother but not always walking with the same rhythm of harmony through the history of mankind?"

NOTES AND SOURCES

[1] The author, Professor Emeritus of Political Science and International Law, is one of the three American members of the International Point Roberts Board appointed by the International Joint Commission in 1971.

[2] For more detail see, International Point Roberts Board *Report to the International Joint Commission on Solutions to the Problems Facing the Residents of Point Roberts* (Ottawa and Washington, October, 1973), Appendix B, 56-58.

[3] #(6), *ibid.*, 57.

[4] *Ibid.*, 56.

[5] See Bellingham, Washington *Herald*, April 24, 1969.

[6] International Joint Commission, "Directive to the International Point Roberts Board," in *Report*, Appendix C, 59-63.

[7] See for this and the total hearings, International Joint Commission United States and Canada, *Public Hearings on the Point Roberts, Washington, Reference*, December 18, 1971 (Allwest-Bemister Reporter, Ltd., Vancouver 16, B.C.).

[8] See "Summary" in *Report*, 1.

[9] State of Washington Laws, 1973, 1st Extraordinary Session, Ch. 110, April 1973: "An Act Relating to Physicians and Surgeons in Emergency Situations . . . "

[10] See *Report*, 34-35. It should also be pointed out that the Washington State Legislature in its Memorial to the Congress of the United States called for the establishment of a commission "to hold a joint conference with the appropriate representative of Canada in order to discuss the problems of Point Roberts, Washington, but not to include territorial or historical rights" (Bellingham *Herald*, April 24, 1969).

[11] *Report*, 43.

[12] *Ibid.*, 2 f. For instance, it has been proposed to transport water by pipeline under Boundary Bay, on the American side of the international boundary, coming from the Blaine area. Yet this very clostly project, while being seriously discussed, has not been given any approval on the part of the American authorities. It is also noteworthy that the lack of sufficient water has resulted in the decision of the Whatcom County authorities not to approve the development of any new subdivision in Point Roberts.

[13] *Ibid.*, 9.

[14] U.S. National Park Service--Parks Canada, *An Inventory of International Park Possibilities: Point Roberts, Boundary Bay, San Juan and Gulf Island Archipelago--A Joint Report Prepared for the International Point Roberts Board* (August, 1973).

[15] *Report*, 44

[16] *Ibid.*

[17] *Ibid.*, 45 ff.

[18] *Ibid.*, 6.

[19] The total account of the hearings can be found in International Joint Commission United States and Canada, *Public Hearing on the Point Roberts, Washington, Reference--Proceedings at Hearing*, volumes 1-5 (Allwest Reporting Ltd., Burnaby 2, B.C.).

[20] The request asked for the additional report by September 15, 1974. For more detail see the *Supplemental Report of the International Point Roberts Board to the International Joint Commission Canada and United States* (September 15, 1974) XXX, 6 f. Also Bellingham *Herald*, April 4, 1974.

[21] *Ibid.*, "Conclusions," 28 ff.

[22] *Ibid.*, 33. See also *News Release* by the IJC by the United States Section, Washington, D.C., November 4, 1974.

[23] Senate Concurrent Resolution No. 14 4 (State of Washington 43rd Legislature, 3d Extraordinary Session).

[24] See the Report of the Select Committee on Point Roberts of the Washington State Senate to the 44th Legislature of January 13, 1975. This Report also includes an "Appendix" of seven items, including the Minutes of the Hearings of the Select Committee, which took place July 25 and 26 at various places.

MICROSPACE GEOGRAPHY: BEGGARS IN
SANTIAGO DE CHILE

J.D. Porteous
University of Victoria

Few geographers have ventured into the realm of microspace. Microspace studies involve the investigation of human behaviour in relation to small spaces and artifacts such as malls, plazas, park benches, tot lots, elevators, supermarkets, and a wide range of rooms from the living room and bathroom to the seminar room and library. Even the human body has its geography, as amply demonstrated in the love poetry of John Donne and, more coarsely, in Shakespeare's *Comedy of Errors*. Until recently, however, geographers have been content to leave the investigation of human behaviour in small spaces to architects, planners, psychologists, and other social scientists (Proshansky *et al.*, 1970). This paper attempts to demonstrate the validity of the geographical study of human behaviour at the microscale.

SIDEWALKS AND BEGGING

The sidewalk has been neglected by geographers as a site for spatial activity. Streets are for traffic, and "The pedestrian remains the largest single obstacle to free traffic movement" (Rudofsky, 1969). However, the sidewalk consists of a series of "behaviour settings" for a variety of urban activities. Where loitering is not forbidden, sidewalks promote social interaction. In the Third World, large numbers of persons live and work on the street; an ongoing research project has found that a considerable proportion of all goods sold in Southeast Asian cities are handled by street traders (McGee, 1974). Street people also provide a variety of essential and useful services, from a shoeshine to prostitution.

The beggar, like the hitch-hiker, also provides a service by easing the conscience of the client while simultaneously bolstering the latter's ego. In urban-industrial nations persons earning their living on the streets have been reduced since the nineteenth century by the creation of standing armies, by rising prosperity by social legislation, and by the actions of private charities (Society for the Supression of Mendicity, 1819). Until the rise of the welfare state and universal automobile use, begging flourished in Western Europe and North America (Fletcher, 1967; Smith, 1970). It remains a major source of livelihood in the Third World.

One of the better manuals on the theory and practice of begging is Bertolt Brecht's *The Threepenny Novel* (1958). Having lost a leg in the Boer War, George Fewkoombey is forced to beg in the streets of London. Before he joins a highly-organized begging operation controlled by Peachum, Fewkoombey learns by trial and error that successful begging involves the recognition of spatial and social regularities.

1. *Attention-getting.* This partly depends upon the ability to excite pity in the observer. Musical instruments are used "to soften people's hearts." Peachum fits up his beggars with suitable props to make them appear destitute and miserable. Serious infirmities may reduce the beggar's ability to attract attention.

2. *Locale.* Regularity of income demands regularity of location, especially in places where there is heavy foot traffic. Fewkoombey is distressed to find that all the best locations are already occupied by Peachum's beggars, who are assigned begging territories which do not overlap.

3. *Microspace niche.* Sidewalks provide the beggar with a range of niches which enable him, with varying degrees of success, to attract attention while at the same time protecting himself from hurt.

A study of the distribution of beggars in Santiago de Chile illustrates the relationship between infirmity type, means of attention-getting, and microspace niche occupance.

BEGGARS IN SANTIAGO DE CHILE

A twice-weekly census of the begging population of downtown Santiago was made over a period of two months during 1970. Frequent rechecking eliminated temporary and transient beggars; the survey was limited to full-time beggars with a fixed "beat." The number of full-time beggars who changed the location of their operations was small, and in most cases involved a regular movement between two or three favoured locations. Observation at fixed intervals yielded data on the land-use at, and the location of, the begging point, the exact position of the beggar on the sidewalk, and the sex, type of infirmity, and approximate age of the beggar, together with his means of attracting the attention of passers-by.

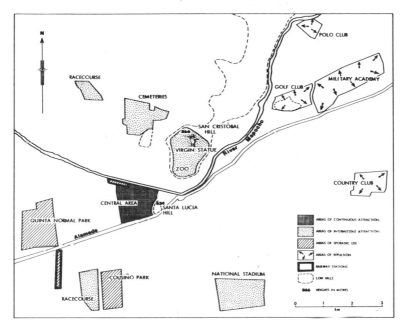

Figure 1

A reconnaissance of Santiago de Chile indicated the infrequent occurrence of begging outside the downtown area (Fig. 1). Parks attracted beggars at weekends, railroad stations during periods of heavy traffic. Sporadic use, depending upon special events, was made of race courses, cemeteries, and the San Cristóbal zoo. Areas attracting no beggars included the elite clubs toward the eastern edge of the city.

Within the downtown area, 50 regularly-occurring begging units, totalling 62 persons, were recognized (Fig. 2). A begging unit consists of a single beggar or a group of beggars working together. The begging population was dominated by males (65 per cent) and the middle-aged; only 16 per cent of the individual beggars were estimated to be under 30, although 29 per cent were judged to be over 60 years of age. Over half the aged persons had no infirmity other than extreme age, and of the ten young beggars six were small children accompanied by adults. In terms of disabilities, the blind were most in evidence (58 per cent), the crippled and the aged each accounted for 18 per cent, and 6 per cent exhibited no obvious infirmity. To attract attention 6 per cent of the beggars sang, and a further 24 per cent played instruments. All these musical beggars were blind, accounting for 41 per cent of all blind beggars. Non-musical mendicants gained attention by exhibiting dependent children or placards bearing the word *ciego* (blind), by rattling metal begging cups, or by verbal appeals.

91

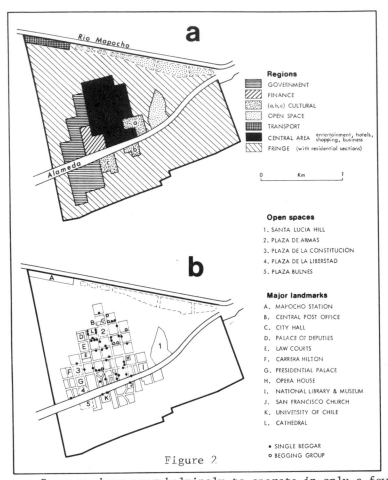

Regions

- GOVERNMENT
- FINANCE
- (a,b,c) CULTURAL
- OPEN SPACE
- TRANSPORT
- CENTRAL AREA entertainment, hotels, shopping, business
- FRINGE (with residential sections)

0   Km   1

Open spaces

1. SANTA LUCIA HILL
2. PLAZA DE ARMAS
3. PLAZA DE LA CONSTITUCION
4. PLAZA DE LA LIBERSTAD
5. PLAZA BULNES

Major landmarks

A. MAPOCHO STATION
B. CENTRAL POST OFFICE
C. CITY HALL
D. PALACE OF DEPUTIES
E. LAW COURTS
F. CARRERA HILTON
G. PRESIDENTIAL PALACE
H. OPERA HOUSE
I. NATIONAL LIBRARY & MUSEUM
J. SAN FRANCISCO CHURCH
K. UNIVERSITY OF CHILE
L. CATHEDRAL

- • SINGLE BEGGAR
- o BEGGING GROUP

Figure 2

Beggars chose overwhelmingly to operate in only a few of the sub-areas of downtown Santiago (Fig. 2; Table 1). The central core, a functionally mixed zone of entertainment, retail, and office facilities, proved to have a density of more than two beggars per block. Wider spacing was evident elsewhere, rates of over 0.4 beggars per block being achieved only in the financial zone and the three cultural areas. Open spaces, either isolated, lacking heavy foot traffic, or full of parked cars, were avoided. Few beggars were found in the government office precinct, which was patrolled by *carabineros*.

Microscale

Within the preferred sub-area, each sidewalk presents a considerable range of environmental niches, varying in their degree

TABLE 1

Location of Santiago Beggars with Regard
to Downtown Sub-areas

Sub-area	Number of Blocks	Number of Beggars	Beggars per Block
Government	15	2	0.15
Finance	5	4	0.80
Cultural	7	3	0.40
Open Space	6	0	0.00
Transportation	1	0	0.00
Central Core	24	52	2.25
Residential Fringe	100	1	0.01

of exposure to pedestrian traffic (Fig. 3). Beggars may choose to
expose themselves immobile on the sidewalk, may walk along it, may
take up positions along the inner sidewalk wall, may retreat to the
more secure shelter of doorway or alcove, or may withdraw into the
safety of deep entrances and arcades. Walls and doorways of eccle-
siastical structures are especially popular. Pablo Neruda, in *Los
Mendigos*, refers to Chilean beggars:

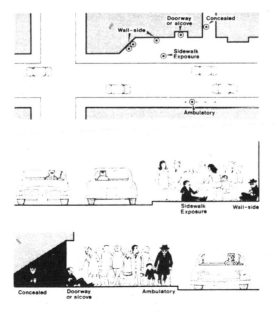

Figure 3

93

By the cathedrals, clotting
the walls . . . grandsons
of church doors . . .

Of the 47 Santiago begging units containing infirm persons,
74.4 per cent chose the wall position, and no more than 4 (8.5 per
cent) chose any other niche (Table 2). Collapsing the data of
Table 2 into wall/non-wall terms, a Chi^2 test showed a significant
difference between the distributions of blind, crippled and aged
beggars at the 0.5 confidence level. To assess differences between
the distributions of the three begging groups over all five available niche types, Goodman and Kruskal's (1954) *tau* was used. Significant independence was found between the distributions of the

TABLE 2

Ecological Niche Choices of Santiago Beggars

	Ambulatory	Exposed	Wall	Alcove or Doorway	Hidden	Total
Blind	2	1	24	1	1	29
Crippled	0	3	4	2	0	9
Aged	0	0	7	1	1	9
	2	4	35	4	2	47

blind/non-blind (0.048), the crippled/non-crippled (0.041), and the
aged/non-aged (0.009). In conjunction with Table 2 one may conclude
that while the majority of beggars favoured the wall as a site for
operations, there was a tendency among the aged to withdraw, while
cripples tended towards exposed positions. The blind were the only
group containing ambulatory members, and the only group to occupy
all five niche types. No significant relationship was found between
sex and niche type.

DISCUSSION

Beggars can be choosers. Before locating at Dives' gate,
Lazarus probably weighed the advantages of all possible locations
known to him. The prime land value intersection of the city is now
an important focus, for beggars locate in response to the heavy
pedestrian traffic of the downtown core.

At the micro-level, differences in environmental preference
and adaption are evident among those Santiago beggars identified as
crippled, blind, or aged. The latter, the group most likely to fear
the bustling sidewalk crowds, exhibit the highest degree of with-
drawal from exposure. In contrast, the blind, 41 per cent of whom

94

play or sing, are able to take up more convenient positions along the inner sidewalk wall. Most cripples, however, are unable to sing or play instruments, and none do so. Consequently, the crippled beggar has no way to attract attention other than by exposing himself to public view. Competition at the wallside by the more adept sonic entreaties of the old and blind therefore forces some of the crippled, relying on visual impact as a means of entreaty, to the center of the sidewalk.

The basic requirements for successful begging appear to be: an obvious physical disability capable of exciting pity in the observer; a container for the collection of coins; and the ability to attract attention by visual or auditory means. The varying ability of the crippled, blind, and aged to perform the last feat, and to withstand the pressures of sidewalk exposure, has resulted in selectivity in the choice of activity-space at the micro-level.

Like all members of sidewalk society, the individual beggar must weigh the financial advantages of exposure to the passers-by against his need for protection from the same hurrying crowd of pedestrians. Depending upon his capabilities and deficiencies, he must then choose one of a range of location options. This preliminary investigation of the selective use by beggars of environmental microspaces is an initial step towards more detailed analyses of the relationships between environment and behaviour on the urban sidewalk.

REFERENCES

Brecht, B. *The Threepenny Novel*. London: Harrison, 1958.

Fletcher, G.S. *London's Pavement Pounders*. London: Hutchinson, 1967.

Goodman, L.A. and W.H. Kruskal. "Measures of association for cross classifications," *Journal of the American Statistical Society*. 49, 1954, 732-764.

McGee, T.G. "Street Traders in Southeast Asian Cities." Paper presented at I.G.U. Regional Conference, New Zealand, 1974.

Proshansky, H.M., W.H. Ittelson, and L.G. Rivlin. *Environmental Psychology*. New York: Holt Rinehart and Winston, 1970.

Rudofsky, B. *Streets for People*. Garden City, N.Y.: Doubleday, 1969.

Smith, J.T. *Vagabondiana*. Los Angeles: Sherwin and Frentel, 1970; facsimile of the 1817 edition.

Society for the Suppression of Mendicity. *First Annual Report*. London, 1819.

CHILDREN'S PERCEPTION OF NEIGHBOURHOOD PARKS:
THEIR REALITY VERSUS OURS

Peter E. Murphy and Linda J. Halliday
University of Victoria

Geography has become a study of the adult world, with scant attention being given to the needs and interests of youth or elderly citizens. Unlike other social sciences, such as sociology and psychology, geography has not developed specific subfields to study these communities, even though they represented 55.4% of Canada's 1971 population.[1] It is important, therefore, that geographers should integrate and compare the views of these groups with the "established" adult interpretations of our world. In this way the world can be viewed from alternative perspectives, the degree of harmony or conflict between these communities can be assessed, and geography can move closer to the holistic discipline[2] it purports to be.

One area where a more comprehensive demographic approach would be desirable is in recreation research. Here, as elsewhere, the emphasis has been on adult and family recreation patterns, while national surveys have indicated that it is the young and elderly who have the major opportunity and participation levels. For example, although the 1972 United States *National Recreation Survey*[3] considered recreation life did not begin until the age of twelve, it found that the "12-17" and "65 or more" age groups had the largest amounts of leisure time, and that the "12-17" group had the highest outdoor recreation participation rate. It is possible, therefore, that the postulates, data, and design criteria associated with outdoor recreation patterns, may not be relevant to the major users or potential participants.

The young and the elderly are the largest users of city parks, yet their views and uses may not coincide with the perceptions and behaviour recorded for adults or family groups, nor necessarily agree with the design and planning criteria that are based on such informa-

97

tion. In one of the few studies of client reaction to neighbourhood parks, Bangs and Mahler[4] noted that children up to the age of twelve (those not surveyed in the ORRRC report) made greater use of the local parks than the adolescents. Furthermore, they noted that most people did not regularly use a local open space if it were further than 400 feet away from their homes, which contrasted to the planned facility range of 650 feet. It is evident that if we are to understand the recreational needs of a whole community, geography must broaden its perspective of the environment and incorporate the perceptions of the young and elderly, particularly in areas where they are major or prominent users.

Since children have had little direct role in the provision and design of local parks, but have been forced to utilize what the adult community feels is appropriate to their interests and development, it would be instructive to examine and compare children's perception of the facilities with that of the official view. Piaget[5] has stated "the child is an alien in an adult world" and this appears to be true in the case of their play world. Recreationists[6] have long recognized that the early and formative years have a direct bearing on an individual's level of outdoor recreation activity in adulthood. Yoesting and Burkhead note:

> The childhood experiences in outdoor recreation activities, then, are another alternative to explain one's adult leisure behavior. An adult is more likely to want to participate in an activity if pleasant memories exist from earlier experiences with that activity. The skills have been learned and the socialization effect has carried over to adult behavior.[7]

Park planners and recreationists have accordingly designed park facilities to encourage these learning and social skills. In the process, however, they may be conditioning the children and limiting their boundless enthusiasm and initiative.

OBJECTIVE

This paper reports on a study that examined the degree to which children's perceptions of local parks were in harmony with the official view of what the parks provided. The children's perceptions were obtained by asking open questions about their local recreation opportunities, and these responses were compared to the local park department's assessment of what was provided in the park system. The two views were compared through the construction of accuracy indices, which expressed the children's perceptions as a relative percentage of the official viewpoint. If a child were in complete harmony with the park department's view he received a score of 100%, and if completely at odds with their view, a zero score. The accuracy indices were treated as dependent variables in an experiment, where the children's age and sex were used to predict the degree of difference in the accuracy indices.

Three specific research hypotheses were examined in the experiment: (1) children's perceptions of their local recreation opportunities will not coincide with the official view, (2) as the children get older, and approach adulthood, their views and the official view will converge, and (3) a sex differentiation will be evident in the perceptual accuracy of the children.

RESEARCH DESIGN AND MODEL

The experiment was conducted in the municipality of Oak Bay, Greater Victoria, during January, 1971. Oak Bay was selected because it is a stable middle-class community that has a good selection of local parks, but not an overwhelming number in terms of a child's imagery. Children from the municipality's second-, fourth-, sixth-, eighth-, and tenth-grades were given structured interviews in a class situation. The interview consisted of open questions regarding the child's use and perception of Oak Bay's park system during the recent Christmas vacation. Each child was then asked to name his or her "most favourite park," and required to list the type of activities they could engage in at that park. The child was also asked to estimate his most favourite park's distance from his home. The final part of the questionnaire was an outline map of Oak Bay, containing the major street pattern and the school locations. On this map the students were asked to locate their most favourite park. In this manner a child's total imagery of the municipal park system was obtained, with an emphasis on the park which he favoured, and presumably knew best.

A hundred completed interviews were obtained from the classroom interviews, and the age and sex distribution of this sample is presented in Table I. The low response rate for the seven year olds

TABLE I

Age and Sex Distribution of Sample

		Age	Sex Male	Female	Total
		7	3	3	6
		9	9	13	22
Experiment	1	7+9	12	16	28
Age	2	11	18	9	27
Levels	3	13	21	2	23
	4	15	10	12	22
Total			61	39	100

99

was caused, in the main, by their inability to locate their favourite park on the map and a low participation rate in the preceding Christmas vacation. The difficulty they had in conveying their perceptions of the local parks confirms Gould's[8] observations in Sweden, where he noted that children of this age had limited information surfaces and formed very constricted mental maps. By the time the children were nine years old, the information surfaces in their mental maps had expanded considerably, but it was between the ages of nine and eleven that the most dramatic filling-in process occurred. Due to the low response rate of the seven year olds in this study and the apparent surge in mental mapping skills after the age of nine, the seven year olds were combined with the nine year olds to form the first age group in the experiment (Table I).

A 4x2 factorial design was used to test the three hypotheses, with age and sex factors being used to predict the values of four perception accuracy indices (Table II). The indices were designed to represent four dimensions of perceptual difference between the official view and the children's perceptions of the park system. They examined Oak Bay's park system in terms of number, activity profile, distance, and location. The *number accuracy* index was obtained by

TABLE II

Research Design for Experiment

			Dependent Variables		
		Number Accuracy	Activity Accuracy	Distance Accuracy	Map Distortion
Factors	1				
	2				
Age	3				
	4				
Sex	1				
	2				

dividing the number of parks each child knew by the official number (20 parks) and expressing this ratio as a percentage. The *activity accuracy* index for the child's favourite park was created by expressing the number of activity options recognized by the child in this park as a relative percentage of the official activities available in the park. The *distance accuracy* to the favourite park was derived by comparing the child's perceived distance between home and this park with the shortest road distance separating the two, and expressed as a relative percentage. The *map distortion* index for the favourite park was obtained placing a half centimeter grid (representing a ground distance of 200 feet) over their maps and noting the number of cells separating their perceived location and the official location.

The age and sex factors used to predict the values of the perceptual accuracy indices were divided into subgroups, or levels. The sex factor had two levels. This division permitted an examination of the different development rates in children. On average, boys:

> tend to excel girls in speed and large body movements, spatial perception, and mechanical aptitude. . . . Girls tend to have slight superiority in memory, language usage, manual dexterity, numerical computation, and perceptual speed.[9]

The age factor was divided into four levels, with the first level representing seven and nine year olds, and the subsequent levels containing the eleven-, thirteen-, and fifteen-year old children. The division of the age factor was based upon Piaget's four major stages of intellectual development in children.[10] According to Piaget:

> the elaboration of space is essentially derived from the coordination of movements so that there is a direct relationship between the development of a sense of space and of sensorimotor intelligence.[11]

He has identified a *sensorimotor stage*, which occurs from birth to two years, where before a child acquires language it is capable of reflex actions and internalized thought. This is followed by a *preoperational stage*, from two to seven years, which heralds the development of preconcepts and language, and is a period when perception rather than logic rules the decision-making process. The *concrete operations stage*, from seven to eleven and a half years, witnesses a decentralization of the child's ego dominance, and the beginning of causal relationship between the child and his environment. At this stage thought is becoming more logical and the child's intellect becomes capable of handling spatio-temporal relationships. The *formal operations stage* occurs from eleven and a half years onwards, and it realizes its frutition in adolescence; it marks the development of reflective thought and deductive reasoning. As in all attempts to partition and classify a continuous process none of the divisions is absolute, and Piaget emphasizes the "how" of the process is more important than the "when."

A Multiple Analysis of Variance[12] was used to analyze the data and test the research hypotheses. Unlike the more common univariate analysis of variance the multivariate technique permits an examination of the factors' effect on the four dependent variables in combination. This is a valuable asset, because though a child may not significantly differ in his relationship to each perceptual accuracy index in isolation, he may differ if the indices were combined into an overall composite index. For example, the difference between a child's perception and the official view may best be described as a combination of his activity accuracy and map distortion rather than by any single index alone. If this is in fact the case a multivariate F test should be significant.[13]

The multivariate analysis of variance compares the perceptual accuracy indices by forming the one linear combination of measures that best discriminates between the age and sex factor levels. That is, a new dependent variable Y_i is calculated and this "derived" variable is a linear function of the scores on the original four indices

$$(Y_i = a_1 X_1 + a_2 X_2 + a_3 X + a_4 X_4).$$

The method may be thought of as testing the effects of the factors on the new variable Y_i. The correlations between the dependent measures are taken into account in the analysis and the confidence region is adjusted accordingly.[14]

In order to meet the multivariate analysis of variance data requirements, a pre-test for normalcy was conducted.[15] It revealed, using Snedecor's[16] sknewness and kurtoris statistics, that the data pertaining to the number accuracy index were normally distributed, while the remaining three indices had positively skewed distributions. Accordingly, the raw data for these three indices were transformed,[17] using a common logarithm transformation, and all the data were standardized.

Though the multivariate analysis of variance programme is relatively insensitive to sample size, the sample sizes should lie between one and two times that of the smallest group.[18] In terms of the thirteen year old girls this criterion was not met. However, since this was only one group of eight it was not considered to be a debilitating constraint, although the results should be interpreted in light of this data limitation.

RESULTS

The multivariate F test for the effects of age and sex on the perceptual accuracy indices is shown in Table III. The age factor was highly significant, with a probability level of less than 0.001, and the sex factor was significant[19] with a probability of 0.047. There was no significant interaction between the two factors, as indicated by the low multivariate F value for age and sex. In terms of the age and sex relationships with individual perception indices, the univariate F tests reveal that age was a significant factor in accounting for number accuracy, while sex was significant in the case of number accuracy and distance accuracy.

The patterns of behaviour for the two factors become clearer on examination of the graphs of their mean scores on the four perceptual accuracy indices. Figure 1 illustrates the mean scores of the two factors on the number accuracy index. It shows that both the

TABLE III

The Effects of Age and Sex on Children's Perceptions
of the Number-, Distance-, Activity-Accuracy,
and Map Distortions of Oak Bay Parks

Source	Univar- iate d.f.	Number Accuracy M.S.	F	Activity Accuracy M.S.	F	Distance Accuracy M.S.	F	Map Dis- tortion M.S.	F	Multi- variate F
Age	3	11.93	18.08**	0.63	0.63	1.77	2.03	0.66	0.86	4.95***
Sex	1	2.46	3.94*	2.00	2.01	4.54	5.20*	0.06	0.08	2.51*
A x S	3	1.08	1.73	0.23	0.23	1.27	1.46	0.19	0.25	0.92

*** p <0.001
* p <0.05

boys and girls knew more parks as they grew older, for both lines move
upward. This indicates that the older children had a more extensive
action space and a greater knowledge of the Oak Bay Park system. In
terms of their activity accuracy (Figure 2), the results show that
there was a general decline in the awareness of activities available
in their favourite park. Both lines decline from the first age level,
although the boys do record a slight increase in activity accuracy at
the age of fifteen. The distance accuracy (Figure 3) reveals the
biggest difference between the two sexes. The girls were consistently
more accurate than the boys in their estimates of the distance separating home and their favourite park, but there was a sharp decline
in their accuracy level between the ages of thirteen and fifteen. The
map distortion (Figure 4) for their favourite park indicates that
both sexes made locational errors when young, but that in general the
distortion became less as they grew older, as illustrated by the
downward slope. It should be noted, however, that the decline was
not consistent in the case of the girls, for there was a marked re-
versal in their trend toward locational accuracy between the ages of
thirteen and fifteen. In fact the girl's mean score at fifteen was
little better than their mean score at eleven years of age.

The results of the multivariate analysis of variance analysis
provide considerable support for the three research proposals of the
study. It is evident that the school children's perceptions of their
local park system do not coincide with the official parks department
view. This can be seen in the low accuracy and high distortion
scores of Figures 1 through 4, inclusive. The young children in particular had very low scores concerning the number of parks that were
available in Oak Bay, and they also made poor estimates of the distance and location for their favourite park.

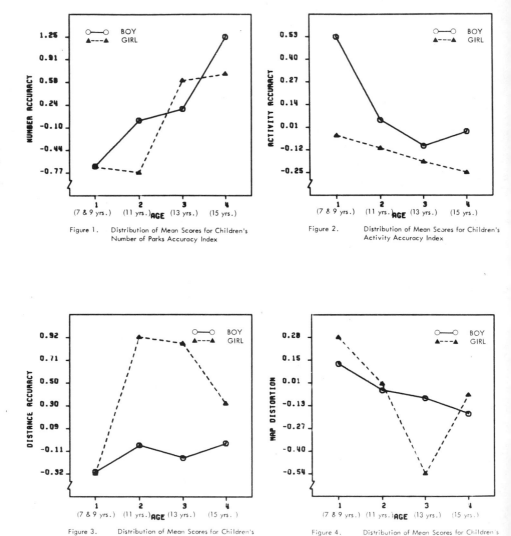

Figure 1. Distribution of Mean Scores for Children's Number of Parks Accuracy Index

Figure 2. Distribution of Mean Scores for Children's Activity Accuracy Index

Figure 3. Distribution of Mean Scores for Children's Distance Accuracy Index

Figure 4. Distribution of Mean Scores for Children's Map Distortion Index.

As predicted in the second research hypothesis, the children's level of accuracy generally improved as they grew older, and their perceptions converged with the official view. But the convergence was neither regular nor universal. In terms of the number accuracy, distance accuracy, and map distortion, there was an erratic convergence of views. Statistical support is given to the visual trend in number accuracy with age (Figure 1) by Table III, which shows that the age factor significantly discriminated the changing perception levels for this index. In the case of the activity accuracy graph (Figure 2) the slope of mean scores indicates a decline in accuracy with age, which is contrary to the expected pattern. A possible explanation for this could be that children over the age of nine are beginning to outgrow certain facilities such as the sandbox and swings, or they are becoming specialized in their recreation through the influence of various sports leagues. In either case they will focus increasingly on fewer facilities and activities within their favourite park.

The third research hypothesis predicted that there would be a sex differentiation in the perceptual accuracy indices, and this is borne out by the graphs and Table III. Boys had better scores in terms of activity accuracy and the girls were consistently better in their distance estimates; in the case of number accuracy and any distortion, the record was mixed. Furthermore, the univariate F tests of variance (Table III) reveal that sex significantly discriminated between the changing perception levels of number-, and distance-accuracy. An interesting point emerges from the graphs in terms of the sex differentiation. The girls always falter at the last age level, regardless of whether their perception indices have been better or worse than the boys up to that point. It is possible that the girls may not be making as much use of the park system by the age of fifteen, compared to their earlier years, and that their perceptual accuracy has deteriorated as a result. If this is so it raises serious questions concerning the adequacy of our park design and recreation programmes for the teenage girl. Are the girls being discriminated against by the emphasis in our parks of outdoor sports utilizing "speed and large body movements," such as soccer and football, to the detriment of more indoor activities which emphasize "manual dexterity," such as badminton, gymnastics and volleyball?

SUMMARY

This study has the limitations of a small sample size and a regional location setting, but its findings have major implications for urban recreation in particular and geography in general. It is evident that children do not perceive and use their neighbourhood parks in the way envisioned or planned by the local municipality. This is particularly noticeable in terms of the activity accuracy index, and the girls' perceptual accuracy by the age of fifteen. Such divergent perceptions indicate that current park design and use is not meeting the interests of our children, and may be a partial cause for the much publicized decline in the physical health of our youth, and society in general. The relevance of the findings to geography is that they clearly indicate that the environmental perspectives of different groups can vary a great deal, even in situations of mutual activity and interest. The official and adult view does not coincide with the children's mental maps or their perceived distances and park activities. Hence if we are to develop a more comprehensive understanding of urban recreation patterns we must be prepared to acknowledge the existence and effect of divergent perspectives. There may not be open conflict between the different recreation communities, but there is certainly a difference of interest and a need to examine and communicate these differences.

ACKNOWLEDGMENTS

The assistance with MANOVA, multivariate analysis of variance computer programme by Dr. Lorne Rosenblood and Ms. Karen Roche of the Department of Psychology, University of Victoria is gratefully acknowledged.

NOTES & SOURCES

[1] Figure arrived at using 1971 census data reported for 0-19 year olds, representing youth, and over 54 year olds, representing elderly. Statistics Canada, *Canada Year Book* (Ottawa, 1973), 212.

[2] R. Hartshorne, *The Nature of Geography* (Chicago: Rand McNally, 1939), 173; D. Harvey, *Explanation in Geography* (Toronto: Macmillan, 1971), 129; R.J. Chorley and P. Haggett, *Models in Geography* (London: Methuen, 1967), 518.

[3] A.L. Ferriss, *National Recreation Survey* (Washington, D.C.: Outdoor Recreation Resources Review Commission Study Report 19, 1962), 361.

[4] H.P. Bangs, Jr., and S. Mahler, "Users of Local Parks," *Journal of American Institute of Planners*, 36, (1970), 330-334.

[5] J. Piaget, *Six Psychological Studies* (New York: Random House, 1967), 47.

[6] W.R. Burch, Jr., "The Social Circles of Leisure: Competing Explanations," *Journal of Leisure Research*, 1, (1969), 125-147; J.C. Hendee, "Rural-Urban Differences Reflected in Outdoor Recreation Participation," *Journal of Leisure Research*, 1, (1969), 333-341; A.J. Sofranko & M.F. Nolan, "Early Life Experiences & Adult Sports Participation," *Journal of Leisure Research*, (1972), 6-18.

[7] D.R. Yoesting and D.L. Burkhead, "Significance of Childhood Recreation Experience of Adult Leisure Behavior: An Exploratory Analysis," *Journal of Leisure Research*, 5, (1973), 28.

[8] P. Gould and R. White, *Mental Maps* (Harmondsworth: Penguin Books, 1974), 133-141.

[9] H.W. Bernard, *Psychology of Learning and Teaching* (New York: McGraw-Hill, 1972), 155.

[10] J. Piaget and B. Inhelder, *The Growth of Logical Thinking from Childhood to Adolescence* (New York: Basic Books, 1959), 16-30.

[11] J. Piaget, *Six Psychological Studies* (New York: Vintage Books, 1968), 14.

[12] D.J. Clyde, *MANOVA: Multivariate Analysis of Variance on Large Computers* (Miami: Clyde Computing Service, 1969).

[13] D.F. Morrison, *Multivariate Statistical Methods* (New York: McGraw-Hill, 1967), 159-206; W.W. Cooley and P.R. Lohnes, *Multivariate Data Analysis* (New York: J. Wiley, 1971), 223-242.

[14] J.C. Holmes, W.F. Throop & L.H. Strickland, "The Effects of Prenegotiation Expectations on the Distributive Bargaining Process," *Journal of Experimental Social Psychology*, 7, (1971), 582-599.

[15] University of Victoria. *SUMMARY: Summary Statistics and Goodness of Fit Tests* (Victoria, B.C.: University of Victoria, Statistics Library, 1974).

[16] G.W. Snedecor, *Statistical Methods* (Ames, Iowa: Iowa State University Press, 1956), 176.

[17] University of Victoria, *UNITRA: Unary Data Transformations* (Victoria, B.C.: University of Victoria, Statistics Library, 1973).

[18] R.L. Hall and P.L. MacNair, "Multivariate Analysis of Anthropometric Data and Classifications of British Columbian Natives," *American Journal of Physical Anthropology*, 37, 1972, 404.

[19] The significant result for the sex factor must be viewed with caution. Subsequent runs of the MANOVA programme, in which all order of entry combinations were used, revealed that the sex factor was not consistently significant. This indicates that order of entry affected the sex factor and its significance, but in all cases the age factor was significant at $p = 0.001$ and the interaction factor was never significant.

RELIGIOUS MERIT AND CONVENIENCE, THE RESOLUTION
OF A CONFLICT WITHIN A PILGRIMAGE THROUGH
SPATIAL-TEMPORAL ADJUSTMENTS

Hiroshi Tanaka
Simon Fraser University

INTRODUCTION

The phenomenon of pilgrimate seems to exist in all major religious traditions.[1] Despite suggestions that the world is becoming increasingly secular, it seems that ever larger numbers of pilgrims are visiting sacred places the world over.[2] This is due partly to the increasing ease with which pilgrimages may be undertaken--in turn being brought about through the symbolic transfer of holy sites to more convenient locations and through the introduction of modern modes of transportation. Yet the traditional practice of journeying by foot to the original holy place or places appears still to be considered by most pilgrims to yield the greatest religious merit. Here it seems a conflict exists between the desire to gain the greatest possible merit from making the pilgrimage and the necessity of completing the journey within the limited time available. This "conflict" symbolizes the larger set of incongruities associated with the increased physical pace of life in secularized societies and the yearning for the security of some sacred absolute.

This paper discusses one particular pilgrimage and considers the ways in which the conflict between religious merit and convenience is at least partially resolved geographically through spatial-temporal adjustment. "Religious merit" here refers to the culturally recognized benefits to be gained through participating in the pilgrimage. The term "convenience" refers to the way in which the journey may be made most efficiently with the least disruption to the routine activities of the individuals involved.

The pilgrimage analyzed here is the Japanese Buddhist pilgrimage to the eighty-eight sacred places located along the periphery

of Shikoku, one of the four major islands of Japan (Figure 1). In
the fall of 1972 and spring of 1973 the author experienced this pilgrimage in the role of participant-observer during research[3] into
the distinctive character of sacred places, and walked most of the
1400 kilometre route that circles the island and links the eighty-
eight sacred places. This pilgrimage is made in the name of Kōbō-
Daishi is believed to have been instrumental in the introduction to
Japan of many new ideas and techniques learned during a period of
study in China.

As in the other great religions, the practice of pilgrimage
to sacred places for spiritual benefit and to render homage is common
in Buddhism, though it was not advocated by Gautama Buddha.[4] It was
not until after the death of Buddha in the sixth century B.C. that
the practice of pilgrimage emerged, probably as his followers, borrow-
ing the idea from Hinduism, began visiting those places throughout
India to which Buddha's ashes were believed to have been distributed
and at which memorial stupas had been erected. Whatever its origin,
the practice of pilgrimage has been widespread in Buddhism for many
centuries, not only in the Mahāyāna school where it is most prevalent
but also in those areas in which Hīnayāna Buddhism dominates.[5] In
Japan, one country in which Mahāyāna Buddhism was adopted, this school
contributed to the establishment of sacred places and the development
of the practice of pilgrimage.

The earliest known reference to Junrei, the Japanese word for
pilgrimage, appears in *Nittō Guhō Junrei-gōki* written by Priest Ennin
after he travelled to China in 838 to study the teachings of Buddhism.
It is commonly thought that the practice of pilgrimage was introduced
to Japan in the mid-Heian Period (794-1192) by Buddhist priests who,
during periods of study in China made pilgrimages to various sacred
places and, on their return, were instrumental in establishing the
practice of pilgrimage in Japan.

Although the origin of the Shikoku pilgrimage is obscure, it
is known that the pilgrimage has been popular since the end of the
sixteenth century. Buddhist writings of the time stress the commonly
held assumption that to spend a lengthy period of time and make the
pilgrimage to the eighty-eight sacred places would bring about im-
measurable religious merit; even to visit only some temples would
bring a reward to pilgrims.[6] It is believed that pilgrims who visit
the eighty-eight sacred places will become free of the eighty-eight
Kenwaku or illusions of the mind that distort the truth and will be
able to attain enlightenment. They will pay homage to the Buddha
whose greatness is divided among the eighty-eight temples, and will
receive the mercy of the various deities.

People of all classes of society--beggars, actors, royalty,
priests, political figures, great teachers, and peasants--have always been present among the pilgrims. The pilgrimage attracts

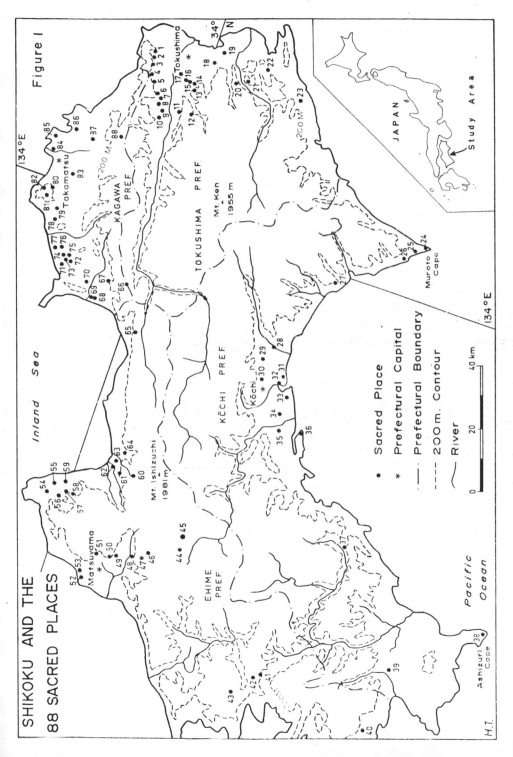

SHIKOKU AND THE 88 SACRED PLACES

Figure I

worshippers from all parts of Japan[7] and from all sects of Buddhism. Truly it is a national phenomenon.

From a sample of 879 ofuda,[8] or calling cards, on which age was indicated, the age range of the present day (1973) pilgrims was determined as from one year to over ninety with the largest age group (25 per cent) being between sixty and sixty-nine years old.[9] These same ofuda revealed that 58 per cent of the pilgrims were female and 42 per cent male.

Following the footsteps of Kōbō-Daishi, pilgrims set out from the first temple situated on the north-east coast of the island, and travel in a clockwise direction around the island. In the past, to make the pilgrimage to the eighty-eight sacred places on foot required about 60 days or longer for the sick and crippled who visited the sacred places hoping to be cured of their afflictions. To make a pilgrimage of two months duration after possibly travelling to Shikoku from other parts of Japan was, for many, impossible. Personal considerations of finances and time were barriers to participation in the pilgrimage and so were political constraints during the Edo Period (1603-1868) that hindered free movement from one prefecture to another and made it necessary for travellers to obtain passports. It was possibly for these reasons that spatial-temporal adjustments were made, permitting the pilgrimage to accommodate a greater number of people.

These spatial-temporal adjustments became apparent during field research in Japan.

LOCATION AND SITE ADJUSTMENTS

Temple Groupings. Perhaps the earliest and most obvious of these adjustments was the gradual emergence of a division of the eighty-eight sacred places into distinct sub-groups. Today thirteen such groups of temples are clearly indicated by special names that have been assigned to them. Nine of these, each of which includes anywhere from five to seventeen temples, may be regarded as the focus of "local" pilgrimages as they primarily attract Shikoku residents. The remaining four groups each encompass all of the temples in one of Shikoku's four prefectures.[10] It is common for pilgrims to call at all of the temples in just one prefecture, and later return to Shikoku several times until all four prefectures have been visited. Thus, through the division of the eighty-eight sacred places into smaller groups, pilgrims have been permitted to make the pilgrimage in convenient segments. With the completion of each segment certain religious merit is believed to have been attained and when all segments of the pilgrimage have been completed the religious merit is almost equal to that gained when the pilgrimage is made all at once.

"Miniature" Pilgrimages Marked by Temples. The emergence of
miniature pilgrimages patterned on the Shikoku pilgrimage would
seem to be another adjustment brought about to facilitate pilgrimage
participation. These miniature pilgrimages to other and less dispersed sets of eighty-eight sacred places, marked by temples, appeared
throughout Japan. The physical area encompassed by each of these
miniature pilgrimages varies widely; some, if made on foot, take two
weeks to complete, while others can be made in one day. In any case,
of at least twenty such miniature pilgrimages[11] established outside
Shikoku, many are still undertaken today (Figure 2). Common to all
miniature pilgrimages is the belief that soil from each of the
original sacred places is embedded in the counterpart of the respective sacred place in each miniature pilgrimage.

"Miniature" Pilgrimages Marked by Stones. In addition to
these twenty miniature pilgrimages, the sacred places of which are
marked by temples, there are throughout Japan, including Shikoku,
numerous miniature pilgrimages of a much smaller scale. In these
the eighty-eight sacred places are represented by a set of stone
markers each of which has carved on it the name of one temple and the
figure of the chief deity of that temple. Very often these stone
markers stand side by side in a row, though sometimes they are spread
over a more extensive area. Often these markers stand within the
temple compound and can be visited in a matter of minutes. They particularly attract the local residents of the area.

The idea of the Shikoku pilgrimage evidently has been diffused throughout Japan for the convenience of those who wish to make
the pilgrimage but who find it difficult to travel to Shikoku and
visit the eighty-eight sacred places. The opportunity provided for
symbolic participation in the Shikoku pilgrimage, affords the participants at least some religious merit. Such miniature pilgrimages
also possibly stimulate the desire to make the so-called Hon-Shikoku,
or the "real Shikoku," pilgrimage in order to attain further religious
merit.

TRANSPORTATION ADJUSTMENT

Modern modes of transportation have affected pilgrimages the
world over by continually expanding their catchment areas[12] and by
making participation easier.

Traditionally, of necessity, the Shikoku pilgrimage was made
on foot but today only a handful of pilgrims walk; the rest travel by
bicycle, train, taxi, private car, or chartered bus, and the time required to complete the pilgrimage is thereby reduced from 60 days to
two weeks. With the reduction in time comes also a reduction in cost.

To make the pilgrimage on foot requires, on the average, between fity and sixty days and is presently the most costly of all the

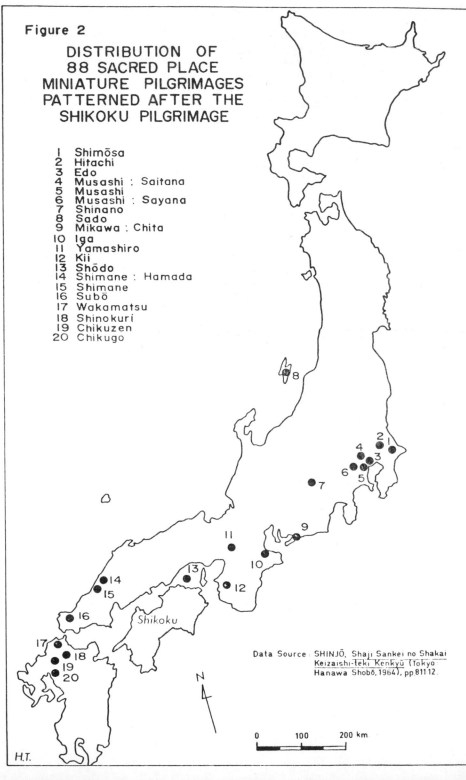

Figure 2

DISTRIBUTION OF
88 SACRED PLACE
MINIATURE PILGRIMAGES
PATTERNED AFTER THE
SHIKOKU PILGRIMAGE

1 Shimōsa
2 Hitachi
3 Edo
4 Musashi : Saitana
5 Musashi
6 Musashi : Sayana
7 Shinano
8 Sado
9 Mikawa : Chita
10 Iga
11 Yamashiro
12 Kii
13 Shōdo
14 Shimane : Hamada
15 Shimane
16 Subō
17 Wakamatsu
18 Shinokuri
19 Chikuzen
20 Chikugo

Shikoku

Data Source : SHINJŌ, Shaji Sankei no Shakai
Keizaishi-teki Kenkyū (Tokyo:
Hanawa Shobō, 1964), pp. 811 12.

N

0   100   200 km

H.T.

ways in which the sacred places may be visited. The average daily
expenses incurred by the walking pilgrim in 1972 totalled approximately 1700 yen.[13] Over a sixty day period the cost would thus be
102,000 yen. The average length of time required to make the pilgrimage by chartered bus is fourteen days. The cost is all inclusive and for about 50,000 yen the pilgrim is supplied with transportation, overnight accommodation, dinner and breakfast for the
duration of the pilgrimage. To make the pilgrimage by taxi costs
approximately 10,000 yen per day but, as this is usually shared by
three or four pilgrims, it is a reasonable way of travelling. The
other expenses incurred would be approximately the same as for a
walking pilgrim, thus the cost of making the pilgrimage by taxi
would work out to be about 50,000 yen per person. Pilgrims travelling
in their own cars generally take longer than those travelling by taxi
due to lack of familiarity with the roads. The daily cost of food and
accommodation would be the same as if the pilgrimage were made on foot
or by taxi and the transportation costs would vary according to the
duration of the pilgrimage and the type of car used. If local buses
and trains are used the pilgrimage takes perhaps thirty days although
there is a wide variation here depending on connections made and how
pilgrims travel to the temples from the nearest point to which public
transportation brings them.

These reductions in the time and expense required to complete
the pilgrimage has increased the frequency with which the pilgrimage
may be made by any one individual, and has thus increased the opportunity to accumulate religious merit.

While it is quite acceptable to use transportation to make
the pilgrimage, it is still believed that the maximum religious merit
will be gained if the pilgrimage is made on foot. Walking pilgrims
are formally referred to as "pilgrims above" while other pilgrims are
referred to as "pilgrims below." Supportive of the belief that it is
preferable to make the pilgrimage on foot is the attempt to keep one
temple in each prefecture accessible only by foot so that pilgrims
may cover at least a small part of the route on foot.[14]

In the past it was of the utmost importance that the temples
be visited in a prescribed order. Today, although the pilgrimage is
still made in a clockwise direction around Shikoku, variation is permitted within the sequential order in which certain temples are
visited to facilitate calling at the temples in the shortest possible
time because the direct route from temple to temple, when wheeled
transportation is used, does not always correspond to the direct
route if the pilgrimage is made on foot.

SPATIAL-TEMPORAL ADJUSTMENT WITHIN THE TEMPLE COMPOUND

At each of the sacred places, certain rituals are performed.
Each particular ritual activity is conducted at a specific place

within the compound: symbolic purification of soul and body at the ablution basin, communication with various deities through hitting the bell, the lighting of candles and incense and the chanting of a sutra (sacred Buddhist text) both at the main hall and at the building dedicated to Kōbō-Daishi. While the majority of pilgrims carry out the prescribed activities, there is wide variation in the time spent by each pilgrim in their performance. Thus it would seem that individual pilgrims make temporal adjustments even within the prescribed rituals.

Priests at the Shikoku sacred places told the author that they note a recent upsurge in participation in the pilgrimage. Does this indicate a rising interest in the pilgrimage, does it simply reflect the increasing ease with which the pilgrimage may be made, or can far more people than ever before now participate actively in the Shikoku pilgrimage? Whatever the case may be, the increasing convenience of the pilgrimage and the substitution of symbolic pilgrimages at more convenient places[15] appear to be connected with an upsurge of pilgrimage activity.

CONCLUSION

This paper has discussed various ways in which the conflict between religious merit and convenience has been met within one particular pilgrimage. A number of spatial-temporal adjustments have been made. First, the series of eighty-eight sacred places has been organized into smaller groups, each of which is the focus of a sub-pilgrimage. Second, the sacred places have been symbolically transferred from Shikoku to other parts of the country through the construction of landscape markers in which symbolic meaning is embodied. Third, the effective travelling time-distance has been reduced through the utilization of modern modes of transportation. Fourth, spatial-temporal adjustments may be made within the pilgrimage ritual as well.

The resolution of the conflict between the desire to achieve religious merit and the need to mould and alter the practice of the pilgrimage to accommodate "contemporary society" would seem to be expressed as an actively developing compromise involving spatial-temporal elements.

NOTES

[1] For a general discussion of pilgrimage that includes Christian, Islamic, and Buddhist practices within the broad context of circulation, see the chapter entitled "Géographie des Pèlerinages" in Pierre Deffontaines, *Geographie et Religions* (Paris: Gallimard, 1948). More specific studies include David E. Sopher, "Pilgrim Circulation in Gujarat," *Geographical Review*, 58, No. 3 (1968), 392-425; Surinder M. Bhardwaj, *Hindu Places of Pilgrimage in India: A Study*

in Cultural Geography (Berkeley: University of California Press, 1973); André Bourgey, "Islam et Geographic," *Revue de Géographie de Lyons*, 45, No. 1 (1970), 75-104; Victor Turner, "The Center Out There: Pilgrim's Goal," *History of Religions*, 12, No. 3 (1973), 191-230.

[2] Turner, *op. cit.*, 195.

[3] Hiroshi Tanaka, "Pilgrim Places: A Study of the Eighty-Eight Sacred Precincts of the Shikoku Pilgrimage, Japan," (unpublished Ph.D. Dissertation, Simon Fraser University, 1975).

[4] Alfred S. Geden, "Pilgrimage (Buddhist)," *Encyclopaedia of Religion and Ethics*, X (New York: Scribner, 1918), 13.

[5] Geden, *op. cit.*, 13.

[6] Jakuhon, *Shikoku Henro Kuodoku-ki*, 1690, I, p. 12, reprinted in *Yoshihiro Kondō, Shikoku Reijō-ki-shū* (Tokyo: Benseisha, 1973), 439-40.

[7] Taku Maeda, *Junrei no Shakaigaku* (Kyoto: Mineruba Shobō, 1972), 174. Maeda states that data concerning a sample of 15,000 pilgrims collected by the priest at Taisan-ji (56) over a twelve month period indicated that all but three (Gunma, Ibaraki, and Fukushima) of Japan's forty-seven administrative regions were represented.

[8] Ofuda, or calling cards, are left by pilgrims at each temple to "eternalize" their visit. On these ofuda pilgrims indicate their age, name, home address, and benefits they hope to receive from making the pilgrimage. It is difficult and often inappropriate to question pilgrims directly, therefore ofuda provide a valuable source of information concerning the participants in the pilgrimage. The author sought and received special permission to examine the ofuda left by pilgrims at two different temples on two different days.

[9] For a more detailed breakdown of age groups see Tanaka, *op. cit.*, 50.

[10] For further discussion of the temple groupings, the sacred places encompassed by each group, the names assigned to the groups, the underlying "symbolic concepts" which support the groupings, the temple groupings, and contemporary practice of the pilgrimage, see Tanaka, *op. cit.*, 172-204.

[11] Tsunezo Shinjō, *Shaji Sankei no Shakai Keizaishi-teki Kenkyū* (Tokyo: Hanawa Shobō, 1964), 811-12.

[12] For example, the Moslem pilgrimage to Mecca stands out for the extent of the area from which worshippers are drawn—from the eastern shore of the Atlantic Ocean to East Asia.

[13] In 1972-73, one Canadian dollar equalled approximately 300 yen.

[14] Recently it has become the practice of pilgrims originating

in a particular part of Hokkaido to travel by chartered bus around
Shikoku but to walk into each temple and to visit only those temples
which are difficult to reach. Many other pilgrims travelling by
chartered bus, if time permits, request that the bus stop a short
distance from each temple so that they may approach the sacred place
on foot.

[15] W. Crook in "Pilgrimage (Indian)," *Encyclopaedia of Religion and Ethics*, X, 25, referred to the fact that Kusinagara, the
scene of Buddha's death, was seldom visited by Lamas and Tibetans
on account of the distance and expense of the journey. Possibly for
the sake of convenience and economy, they transferred the site of
Buddha's death from Kusinagara to a place known as Salkusa in Assam.
Much more recently, Vatican officials announced that for the first
time Roman Catholics can obtain an indulgence, that is remission of
punishment for past sins, by making local pilgrimages rather than
going to Rome for the 1975 Holy Year. Each country will be able to
nominate local churches or cathedrals for pilgrimages. "Vatican
Alters Remission Method for Pilgrims," *Vancouver Province*, November
5, 1974.

THE DEVELOPMENT OF COMMUNITY PASTURES IN SASKATCHEWAN: A CASE STUDY IN THE DEVELOPMENT OF LAND POLICY

Peter Laut
Division of Land Use Research, CSIRO, Australia

ABSTRACT

This paper identifies the origins and development of the Community Pastures system in Saskatchewan between 1908 and 1939. It is divided into four sections:

(a) A discussion of the early settlement of south-western Saskatchewan and the perception of environmental limitations on wheat cultivation in this region which led to the Better Farming Conference held at Swift Current in 1920 and the subsequent Royal Commission of Inquiry into farming conditions in the Province of Saskatchewan;

(b) The development of the concept "community pasture" and the two models, "Matador" and "Nashlyn" developed under the guidance of F.H. Auld;

(c) The transfer of Crown Lands to the Provincial Government, the Land Utilization Act of Saskatchewan--the operational legislation for the programme for better land use in the Province--the Prairie Farm Rehabilitation Act, and the development of the PFRA Community Pastures in conjunction with the Land Utilization Board;

(d) The expansion of all three types of community pasture in Saskatchewan--the PFRA, the Provincial, and the Cooperatives--from 1939 to 1969.

INTRODUCTION

The purpose of this paper is to demonstrate the interplay of environment, personality and economic circumstances in the development of policy towards land resources marginal for arable farming in Saskatchewan. One mechanism for implementing marginal land policy in Saskatchewan has been the community grazing system, and the development of this system is used as the vehicle for examining the importance of different sets of factors at different points in time.

The expansion of arable farming in the Canadian Prairies and especially in Saskatchewan was indissolubly tied to wheat cultivation. However, it was clearly recognized by the turn of the century that wheat monoculture was undesirable and the leaders of the agricultural community and the Saskatchewan Department of Agriculture authorities were concerned to have a stable rural economy involving a variety of crops and a significant livestock component. This concern was based not only on the undesirability of dependence upon wheat as the only source of income, but also on the need to develop rotations to preserve soil texture and fertility. Nowhere in Saskatchewan was the need for a mixed farming system greater than in the south-west. In 1908 wheat yields fell below 10 bushels per acre in Crop District 3 and 10.5 bushels in Crop District 4 (Table 1 and Figure 1).

TABLE 1

Wheat Yields in South-Western Saskatchewan, 1907-1915

| | Crop Districts | | | | |
	2	3	6	mean for 2, 3, 6	mean for Saskatchewan
1907	15.6	17.8	16.1	15.4	13.5
1908	17.6	9.8	10.3	15.1	13.7
1909	24.7	28.5	23.9	25.1	22.1
1910	19.4	10.9	7.5	14.7	15.6
1911	21.2	16.8	16.8	19.1	18.5
1912	23.0	21.7	21.5	20.3	19.9
1913	22.0	17.0	18.0	19.9	19.5
1914	13.0	2.0	10.0	9.9	12.4
1915	26.2	31.0	30.3	28.4	25.2

These low yields were attributed to poor soil preparation, which it was thought could be overcome by superior cultivation techniques. Indeed, the following year the crop was excellent with means of 28½ bushels for Crop District 3 and 25 for Crop District 4, which encouraged further expansion of wheat cultivation. From 1910 to 1913 wheat yields were moderate to high throughout most of settled Saskatchewan, but in general the 1914 wheat crop was a failure in western

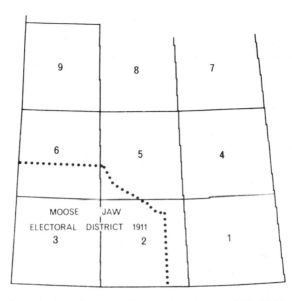

Figure 1. Saskatchewan: Crop Districts 1908–1915, and
Moose Jaw Electoral District, 1911.

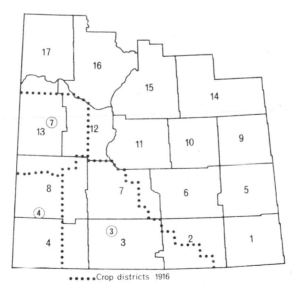

•••••Crop districts 1916

Figure 2. Saskatchewan: Census Divisions and Crop
Districts in South Western Saskatchewan, 1916.

121

and south-western Saskatchewan. These districts as a whole achieved
a mean yield of less than 10 bushels per acre, but Crop District 3
reported a disastrous mean yield of some 2 bushels per acre. The
effect of this one year of very low yield was to emphasize the precarious nature of some wheat farming communities in the Province.
This prompted a further and more realistic appraisal of the farming
system and of the need to introduce some elements of mixed farming
into the economy.

        In 1911, occupied land in the Electoral District of Moose
Jaw (Figure 2), which comprised 21.6 million acres in the south-
western corner of the Province, totalled only 8.1 million acres or
37.3% of its total area, whilst improved and cropped land totalled
2.0 million acres and 1.4 million acres, or 9.4% and 6.6% respectively
of the total land area of the Electoral District. These data indicate
that there were considerable areas of unoccupied land and suggest that
there must have been considerable idle land among the occupied areas,
especially in those Rural Municipalities where the Herd Law was en-
forced. By 1916, 55% of the total area of the four Census Divisions,
which together approximate the Moose Jaw Electoral District of 1911,
was occupied farmland, 49% of this was improved land and 35% had been
under field crops the previous year. By 1931 the agricultural lands
of the south-west were almost totally occupied, to the extent of 85%,
with 52% of occupied land improved and 33% under crop. Much of the
land then occupied was eventually to prove sub-marginal for arable
farming, and contemporary reports suggest that considerable areas of
land suited for grazing livestock were unused because of Herd Law
enforcement.

        In 1915, the wheat crop was excellent throughout Saskatchewan,
and of "bumper"proportions in the south-west. There is little doubt
that this harvest and those of the next few years allayed settlers'
fears about the suitability of the environment of the southwest wheat
production. Then in 1919 the harvest for the same districts was disastrous, averaging 5.5 bushels per acre for the south-west and as low
as 3.5 for the extreme south-west--Crop District 4 (Table 2).

TABLE 2

Wheat Yields in South-western Saskatchewan, 1916-1920

		Crop Districts		mean for	mean for
	3	4	7	3, 4, 7	Saskatchewan
1916	15.6	18.1	18.0	15.8	14.2
1917	12.6	12.3	16.2	13.6	14.2
1918	8.1	4.7	5.2	6.7	10.0
1919	5.8	3.5	6.8	5.6	8.5
1920	11.0	9.9	13.8	11.5	11.2

Community leaders organized a conference of farmers and agriculturalists to assess the agricultural potential of the lands of south-western and western Saskatchewan, and to demonstrate the need for agriculturalists to provide a satisfactory system of farming which would allow the agricultural community some leeway in periods of drought. This conference, held at Swift Current in July 1920, became known as The Better Farming Conference and resulted in the Royal Commission of Inquiry into farming conditions in the Province of Saskatchewan which issued its findings the following year. The areas of investigation for the Commission included:

1. The grazing land situation, including the need for, the advantages of, and the possibilities for, community grazing;

2. The control and prevention of soil drifting and reclamation of drifted soils;

3. The desirability and possibility of moving settlers from inferior to better lands;

4. The development of a system of farm management suited to south-western Saskatchewan;

5. The need for further experimental work on arable farming;

6. The means and methods of extending agricultural knowledge throughout the country.

The Secretary for this Commission was H.F. Auld, a young and energetic administrator, who had become Acting Deputy Minister for the Department of Agriculture for Saskatchewan in 1915, and Deputy Minister in 1917. Just how much influence this Royal Commission had on Auld is difficult to determine, but the Commission consisted of some of the more notable agriculturalists of the west, including: W.D. Rutherford, Dean of the College of Agriculture, Saskatoon; John Bracken, President of the College of Agriculture, Winnipeg; George Spence, Member of the Saskatchewan Legislative Assembly, farmer, and later an officer in the Dominion Department of Agriculture and the Prairie Farm Rehabilitation Authority; and Neil McTaggart, Member of the Saskatchewan Legislative Assembly, farmer, and later Provincial Minister for Agriculture and Deputy Minister of the Dominion Department of Agriculture.

It is apparent in retrospect that many of the ideas concerning land policy and utilization for the sub-marginal lands of Saskatchewan presented in the Commission report were carried forward and developed by Auld during the following thirty years.

123

From its first meeting, it seems evident that the Commission was pre-disposed towards a farming system involving livestock (most likely cattle) as well as wheat cultivation. Although the Dominion Department of the Interior, Lands and Forest Branch, had devised a system of cooperative leasehold which it had been encouraging landholders to utilize on its reserve lands at about this time, it might be considered that the Commission provided the necessary body of opinion to develop the embryo into a practical form of community grazing which could be employed as part of the overall farming system, primarily in western Saskatchewan but also wherever submarginal areas were sufficiently large to justify pasture development. Concurrently, the Commission gathered data on costs involved in using land held under various forms of lease and title for grazing. These demonstrated very convincingly that grazing could be practiced economically only on leased public lands, largely because of the nature of land assessment and resulting tax rates.

COMMUNITY PASTURE

In the context of south-western Saskatchewan, the Commissioners saw the "community pasture" as an ideal alternative to an increase in farm area for they considered that it was absolutely imperative to increase the land resources available to individual farmers. From the technological point of view, the Commission could see a number of advantages accruing to community grazing areas, as opposed to individual grazing holdings.

However, whilst the Commission was prepared to promote the legal basis for establishing community pastures, it maintained that the onus of seeking land for the community pastures, and of organizing, establishing, and managing them rested with the farming community. In this way, it sought to keep government involvement to a minimum in establishing and administering community pastures.

The Matador Lease and Community Pasture

The Dominion Government responded cautiously to the recommendations of the Royal Commission. The Deputy Minister of the Department of the Interior visited the west early in 1922, at which time he negotiated conditions relating to community grazing on Dominion lands in Saskatchewan. These conditions were later embodied in the Dominion Government Order-in-Council, April 12th, 1922, in which it was obvious that the Dominion Government was gradually changing its position on grazing leases. In particular, the Government of Saskatchewan was given first opportunity to renew leases of grazing lands for community grazing purposes.

Coincidentally, a large leasehold of grazing land known as the Matador Ranch became available for provincial lease from the Dominion Government. The Matador Land and Cattle Company, a firm

124

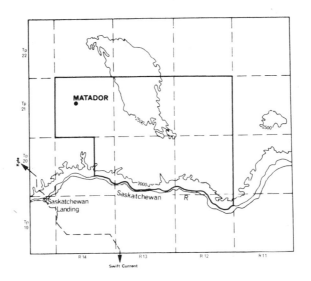

Figure 3.   Location of the Matador Ranch
and Community Pasture.

based on Scottish capital and operating from working headquarters at
Trinidad, Colorado, U.S.A., had obtained a lease of approximately
125,000 acres of land in south-western Saskatchewan (Figure 3).

Auld appears to have been particularly anxious to use this
lease as a community pasture. As early as July 1921, Auld had
written to a group of farmers at Waldock who had indicated their interest in obtaining a portion of the Matador lease for community
grazing, suggesting that they might not only gain an advantage towards acquiring such a lease by writing to the Department of the
Interior, but would assist the same Department to reach a general
decision concerning community grazing by indicating that they had
formed an association under the Agricultural Cooperative Association
Act of Saskatchewan.

There were also notable pressure groups against the development of the Matador into a Community pasture; ranchers, both large
and small were anxious to obtain the lease lands and the Council of
Rural Municipality 226, "Victory," made extravagant claims to have
the lease thrown open for settlement. However, Auld made it clear to
all concerned that he would not prejudice the opportunity of obtaining the lease by attempting to develop it other than through the 1922
Order-in-Council. As to the type of Community Pasture development for
the Matador lands, Auld indicated that there were at least two options

under consideration: either subdivide it into about four district divisions and lease them to farmers' associations, or maintain it as a unit and place a manager in charge to organize the pastures' operation. Eventually circumstances forced Auld to accept the latter procedure; a manager was appointed and the Matador Community Pasture began operations.

In effect the Matador was the first true community pasture and through its day-to-day operations most of the guiding principles for the operation of later Provincial and Prairie Farm Rehabilitation Authority (P.F.R.A.) pastures were developed. Basically, the issue of apportionment of costs, responsibility of the pasture to stock owners, and the extent of stock owner involvement were the main concerns. In all, the Matador provided an excellent basis for the later development of the P.F.R.A. and the Provincial pasture systems. However, it was but one of several possible alternate community grazing models.

The Nashlyn Livestock Association and Pasture

The Nashlyn Livestock Association, which was incorporated under the Agricultural Cooperative Act in 1923, provided an obvious alternative to the Matador approach to community pastures, and one, by the sympathy shown in his correspondence, Auld clearly approved. In this case, the farmers of the Nashlyn district, under the guidance of the local agricultural representative, incorporated themselves under the Agricultural Cooperative Act, and through the provisions of the 1922 Dominion Order-in-Council and the Provincial Grazing Lands Act 1923 obtained a lease of 56,680 acres of grazing land (Figure 4).

The Nashlyn Livestock Association and its pasture were similar to a number of other associations which came into being for the same purpose. Some were stillborn, some succeeded for a few years, and a few such as Nashlyn succeeded for many years and became established Provincial or P.F.R.A. pastures, or remained as successful cooperative pastures. In the case of stillborn associations it was frequently not so much a lack of local leadership, but an unwillingness to make long-term commitments involving capital, labour, and responsibility on the part of the local community.

The development of the Nashlyn Association laid down many of the principles for the operation of cooperative pastures. The aims and purposes of such associations were not self-evident, despite by-laws; public opinion was often poorly informed and prone to prejudice; entitlement to use such pastures and relationships among associations were anything but well defined and required time to develop. It seems that the Nashlyn pasture started well. The Agricultural Representative for the Robsart District reported that the initial meetings of the Association clearly represented a cross-section of the local community and were open to entry by anyone who was prepared to shoulder the necessary financial responsibilities for improvements.

126

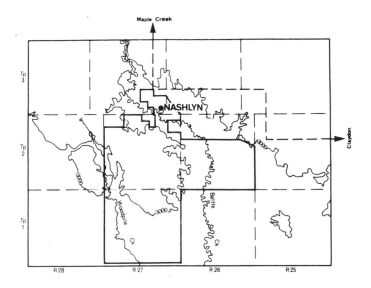

Figure 4. Location of the Nashlyn
Community Pasture.

Department of Agriculture records indicate that somehwere
between eight and ten livestock association pastures existed between
1922 and 1935. Some were extremely shortlived and never actually
functioned, others functioned for only a few years. Nashlyn Association Pasture, despite its precarious financial situation in the mid-
1930's, went on to become one of the first of the P.F.R.A. pastures
in the late 1930's.

GOVERNMENT LEGISLATION

*The Transfer of Crown Lands to the
Province and the Land Utilization Act*

Between 1922 and 1929 it could be said that the demand for
community pastures did not expand significantly. Wheat yields
throughout this period were not particularly low and in several years
were quite high (Table 3).

This appears to have placed a brake on the expansion of the
livestock industry and the consequent demand this would have generated
for community pastures. From information available it seems that in
these early years of operation the Matador did not receive as much
support from nearby farming communities as it might have done and
there was some surplus capacity. On the other hand, despite encour-

127

agement from the Department of Agriculture district representatives, only a few livestock associations managed to develop operative pastures and to maintain these successfully.

TABLE 3

Wheat Yields in South-western Saskatchewan, 1921-30

| | | Crop Districts | | | |
	3	4	7	mean for 3, 4, 7	mean for Saskatchewan
1921	15.1	9.2	14.2	13.7	14.8
1922	24.3	18.8	12.3	**20.2**	20.3
1923	19.5	16.8	26.0	20.6	19.8
1924	18.9	6.8	5.6	10.5	10.2
1925	17.7	9.8	21.3	17.1	18.5
1926	15.8	8.8	12.4	13.7	16.2
1927	14.6	22.7	17.3	16.7	16.4
1928	25.8	27.1	24.0	25.5	23.3
1929	6.8	13.2	12.1	9.4	11.1
1930	8.0	13.1	18.9	13.4	13.7

While the late 1920's were years for gaining experience and in a limited sense, for consolidating the community pasture models, the early 1930's provided events of temendous significance to the Provincial Government's policy towards marginal lands. First, in 1930 natural resources including land came under the jurisdiction of the Provincial Government, allowing the opportunity for closer implementation of land policy regarding marginal and submarginal lands; second, the Great Depression severely affected the economic status of the Prairie farmer through its impact on the British market for wheat and beef; and third, a series of devastating droughts in the south and west of the province severely altered the perception of the land resource and called for notable readjustment of the agricultural system of south-western Saskatchewan.

Undoubtedly the depression made the drought years appear more devastating, but in terms of regional wheat yields only the seasons from 1929 to 1938 were exceedingly difficult in most parts of Saskatchewan (Table 3 and 4). The Province was by no means capable of handling the doubly difficult crisis and the Federal Government became involved in the rehabilitation of the Western Provinces, especially Saskatchewan. In turn, this meant that, although the Provincial Government obtained control of the land resources in Saskatchewan in 1930, much of the consequent land policy concerning submarginal agricultural lands was developed in association with the Federal Government.

TABLE 4

Wheat Yields in South-western Saskatchewan, 1931-1940

	3	4	7	mean for 3, 4, 7	mean for Saskatchewan
			Crop Districts		
1931	2.4	5.0	12.7	5.8	8.2
1932	7.7	15.1	16.3	11.5	13.0
1933	3.7	4.0	3.8	3.8	8.4
1934	3.6	4.3	8.6	5.3	8.6
1935	11.0	6.7	10.1	9.9	10.2
1936	4.7	1.3	5.3	4.3	8.0
1937	0.2	0.1	1.4	0.5	2.7
1938	6.6	9.5	11.2	8.5	9.6
1939	16.6	16.4	19.3	17.4	17.6
1940	16.5	19.9	22.1	18.8	17.5

Land resources became the responsibility of the newly created Department of Natural Resources, which administered the Provincial Lands Act as well as the Forest Act, the Water Rights Act and the Water Power Act, all of 1930-31. No doubt the breadth of the scope of this Department and the separation of Agriculture from Land Resources limited Auld's influence on land policy. However, after five years of droughts of varying intensities in the south and west of Saskatchewan and concomitant wind erosion in many of the light soils districts, the Land Utilization Bill was presented to the Saskatchewan parliament and was assented to in February 1935. At this time I. McTaggart, a former member of the 1920 Royal Commission, was the Minister for Agriculture to whom Auld was responsible, and the connection between the findings of the 1920 Royal Commission and the Land Utilization Act was very direct. Briefly, the Land Utilization Act created the Land Utilization Board. This Board had the right to declare an area of land as unsuitable for agriculture (i.e., arable farming) and such lands then became public lands to be utilized in a manner to benefit the residents of the area; this was a bold move designed to provide the legal means to rehabilitate both land and men in districts for sub-marginal land resources.

The P.F.R.A. and the Early Development of
the P.F.R.A. Community Pastures System

The Province might provide the legal means to implement a land retirement and rehabilitation policy, but in the 1930's it lacked the economic means to put the policy into operation. Without financial capability the Land Utilization Act was toothless. Gardiner, the Federal Deputy Minister for Agriculture, who recognized the weakness of the situation, did much to promote the Frairie Farm Rehabilitation Act (1935). The initial P.F.R. Act did not include land utilization and land settlement within its scope but the subsequent amended agreement in 1937 provided for both and allowed an interpretation which included the development of community pastures as part of land rehabilitation. The keystone to the implementation of the P.F.R. Act were the agreements, first signed in January 1937, between the Saskatchewan and Dominion Governments. In summary, the more important sections of the agreements referred specifically to:

1. The *Area* in which the Acts and agreements were operative;

2. The method of procedure to initiate pasture, irrigation, and other projects;

3. The responsibility of the Province for providing title for lands to be included in particular projects.

The area in which the Acts and agreements were operative did not include all of Saskatchewan (Figure 5).

The boundary was defined in a most arbitrary manner by including all local government areas which the Advisory Committee Members considered to be prone to drought. As far as the initiation of pasture development was concerned the Provincial and Rural Municipality authorities were supposed to submit details of the required projects which the P.F.R.A. authorities would consider and in turn act upon. However, it seems that by the time the first agreement was signed the Land Utilization Committee already had a number of possible locations for pastures under consideration. Many of these locations were known to require considerable rehabilitation (Figure 5).

In 1934 a number of cooperative pastures were operating under the guidance of the Dominion Department of Forestry in southwestern Saskatchewan and the Matador Provincial Pasture was being operated by the Saskatchewan Department of Agriculture. There were a total of seven pastures which could be labelled "community pastures" and these included some 172,795 acres of land (Figure 6 and Table 5). Once the P.F.R.A. began its operations in association with the Land Utilization Board, community pasture projects went ahead rapidly.

In some cases where it was impossible to make contact with absentee owners, private lands were included to round out community pasture holdings and it was many years before title to such holdings was obtained. Although in the early Advisory Committee Meetings, Gardiner indicated that the rehabilitation of farmers was an important aspect of P.F.R.A. projects, the actual development of comunity pastures seemed to be much more oriented to land rehabilitation.

Figure 5.   Saskatchewan: Northern boundary of
             P.F.R.A. activities and sites considered
             for community pastures prior to 1935.

□   **P.F.R.A. pastures**
△   **Provincial pastures**
○   **Cooperative Grazing Association pastures**
■▲● **newly developed**
□△○ **previously developed**

Key for Figures 5-13.

There were some movements of families from acknowledged submarginal
lands but their numbers were not great.   The selection of actual
pasture locations was based on a number of rationales: Nashlyn Livestock Association Pasture was merely taken over and improved in
return for cancelling unpaid tax and lease fees, Mariposa was established through the offices of the Rural Municipality Council, and
others were located simply because large areas of submarginal land
were available.

      By 1939 P.F.R.A. pastures enclosed 576,800 acres of sub-
marginal land in twenty-four pastures.   The majority of these were

Table 5

Areas of P.F.R.A., Provincial and Cooperative Community

Pastures by Census Divisions, 1934-1969

Census Divisions	Type	1934	1939	1944	1949	1954	1959	1964	1969
1.	P.F.R.A.	–	12,740	12,740	32,020	46,800	54,140	55,100	55,898
	Prov.	–	–	–	–	–	–	–	1,699
	Coop.	–	–	–	–	–	–	–	–
2.	P.F.R.A.	–	68,880	116,600	149,680	173,840	189,095	189,095	189,098
	Prov.	–	–	–	11,200	27,000	27,000	15,800	15,800
	Coop.	–	–	–	–	2,310	2,310	13,726	18,106
3.	P.F.R.A.	–	15,520	33,120	34,320	41,200	21,940	41,940	42,020
	Prov.	–	–	–	7,840	13,455	42,245	44,070	55,051
	Coop.	–	–	–	–	9,145	16,206	17,624	23,222
4.	P.F.R.A.	–	174,600	451,740	460,000	469,640	484,720	488,240	488,240
	Prov.	–	–	–	25,600	37,792	39,960	49,560	60,955
	Coop.	26,755	26,755	38,599	62,161	72,713	120,229	121,039	125,698
5.	P.F.R.A.	–	–	41,200	41,520	60,490	59,760	93,129	99,877
	Prov.	–	–	–	–	–	–	–	6,951
	Coop.	–	–	–	–	636	636	636	7,267
6.	P.F.R.A.	–	–	–	–	–	–	1,450	1,450
	Prov.	–	–	–	4,720	4,270	5,760	5,760	10,182
	Coop.	–	–	–	–	804	804	804	804
7.	P.F.R.A.	–	41,680	100,680	100,620	106,800	107,100	107,100	103,580
	Prov.	58,195	58,195	58.195	41,892	81,907	86,927	87,727	107,730
	Coop.	–	–	–	4,207	10,319	44,680	54,209	54,464

cont.

Table 5 - Page 2

Census Divisions	Type	1934	1939	1944	1949	1954	1959	1964	1969
8.	P.F.R.A.	-	70,880	112,140	148,460	183,160	213,350	206,070	206,070
	Prov.	58,195	58.195	58.195	33,892	75,287	90,287	91,247	97,096
	Coop.	23,850	23,850	28,170	34,111	68,401	68,401	90,968	92,003
9.	P.F.R.A.	-	-	22,080	22,080	22,080	22,080	54,720	52,800
	Prov.	-	-	-	-	-	-	16,320	55,416
	Coop.	-	-	-	-	-	-	-	-
	P.F.R.A.	-	-	22,080	22,080	22,080	53,620	64,660	66,740
	Prov.	-	-	-	631	631	4,792	9,619	10,397
	Coop.	-	-	-	-	-	-	-	-
11.	P.F.R.A.	-	58,640	76,080	76,720	124,080	131,440	131,870	144,510
	Prov.	-	-	-	-	-	-	-	8,080
	Coop.	-	-	-	640	640	640	640	-
12.	P.F.R.A.	-	31,460	33,520	29,820	42,880	43,880	44,800	44,800
	Prov.	-	-	-	-	8,800	8,800	8,800	9,107
	Coop.	5,800	5,800	5,800	5,800	34,650	50,076	52,583	56,516
13.	P.F.R.A.	-	115,160	135,800	149,240	188,000	190,269	192,409	196,307
	Prov.	-	-	-	-	-	-	-	8,307
	Coop.	-	-	-	-	99,680	112,576	115,679	117,570
14.	P.F.R.A.	-	-	-	-	-	-	8,160	13,973
	Prov.	-	-	-	-	-	31,813	50,533	63,212
	Coop.	-	-	-	-	-	1,280	5,248	3,686
15.	P.F.R.A.	-	-	-	-	-	-	-	5,884
	Prov.	-	-	-	-	-	-	-	11,953
	Coop.	-	-	-	-	2,653	3,249	6,596	10,110

cont.

Table 5 - Page 3

Census Divisions	Type	1934	1939	1944	1949	1954	1959	1964	1969
16.	P.F.R.A.	-	-	-	-	64,960	65,120	119,040	119,200
	Prov.	-	-	-	-	16,520	36,920	38,574	54,834
	Coop.	-	-	-	-	14,468	30,223	39,920	53,150
17.	P.F.R.A.	-	-	20,960	19,698	22,733	24,480	24,480	24,480
	Prov.	-	-	-	-	-	-	5,760	16,944
	Coop.	-	-	-	9,131	19,794	22,433	16,799	16,799
18.	P.F.R.A.	-	-	-	-	-	-	-	-
	Prov.	-	-	-	-	-	-	14,639	24,982
	Coop.	-	-	-	-	2,800	2,800	-	-

1934

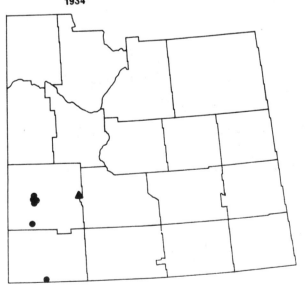

Figure 6.   Location of Community Pastures, 1934.

1939

Figure 7.   Location of Community Pastures, 1939.

located in Census Divisions 2, 4, 11, and 13. All the new pastures
were large, averaging some 24,600 acres in area, and the three
pastures in Census Division 4 totalled 176,600 acres and extended
almost 40 miles in a contiguous strip along the Montana/Saskatchewan
border (Figure 7). P.F.R.A. pastures, although enclosing more than
one-half million acres of land on which widespread soil drifting was
known to have occurred, did not at this time include a very high proportion of eroded areas. Between 1939 and 1944 the total area under
community pastures almost doubled to 1.37 million acres in 57 separate pastures. Only one of the new pastures was not P.F.R.A. controlled and 48% of the new acreage was located in Census Division
4, particularly to the south of Cadillac in the vicinity of Beaver
Valley, Val Marie and Mansfield. Other new pastures were widely
scattered in Census Divisions 2, 5, 7, 8, 9, 10, 11 and 17 (Figure 8).

At the end of 1944 1.6 million acres of submarginal agricultural land were included in community pastures. However, submarginal land was no longer widely available in blocks of 15,000
acres or more (the minimum area required by the P.F.R.A. to establish
a pasture) in a patent form readily accessible to the Saskatchewan
Crown. Land Utilization Advisory Committee and Land Utilization
Board correspondence suggests that the lack of available land began to cause friction, especially as there was land available outside the P.F.R.A. "Area," which could not be utilized because of

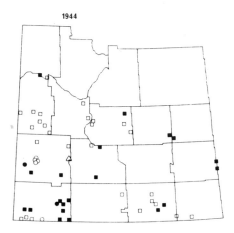

1944

Figure 8. Location of Community Pastures, 1944.

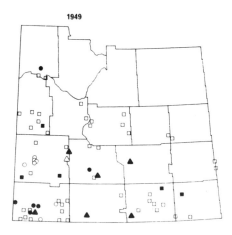

1949

Figure 9. Location of Community Pastures, 1949.

its location. Yet at the same time the P.F.R.A. Branch was not in-clined to extend the "Area" despite very favourable discussions in the Land Utilization Advisory Committee.

EXPANSION OF THE COMMUNITY GRAZING SYSTEM

The period 1945-1949 was one of relative stagnation in the development of the Saskatchewan community pastures. Whereas approx-imately 600,000 acres of land had been incorporated in community pastures in each of the two previous five-year periods, only 163,000 were incorporated in 1945-49. This was mainly in Provincial Pastures with a small area in some new Cooperative Grazing Association Pas-tures, all of which were still located within the P.F.R.A. "Area" (Figure 9).

Nineteen new pastures were brought into use between 1945 and 1949. Six of these were new Provincial pastures and a further six were cooperative pastures. The new Provincial and cooperative pas-tures were much smaller than those of the P.F.R.A. with mean areas of 1,900 and 6,600 acres respectively compared with 26,900 acres for new P.F.R.A. pastures.

The differences between the Saskatchewan Provincial L.U.B., responsible for acquiring land suitable for the P.F.R.A. pastures, and the P.F.R.A. Land Utilization Advisory Committee were increased by the negotiation of an agreement between the Dominion and Manitoba Governments in which Manitoba retained title to lands used in pas-tures. Eventually a new agreement was signed in 1949 which enabled the Saskatchewan Crown to retain title to all new P.F.R.A. community pasture developments, but the Provincial L.U.B. remained responsible for providing the Dominion Crown with title for all lands included in pastures commenced before December 1944. At this time the limi-tations of the P.F.R.A. "Area" were also abandoned.

This did not mean that the Provincial pasture system would not continue to expand. There were now three elements in the Saskatchewan community pasture system: P.F.R.A. pastures which would continue to develop blocks of submarginal lands in excess of 15,000 acres (although later this was dropped under special circumstances), the Provincial segment which included both small and large pastures, and a spate of small cooperative pastures.

The period 1950-54 was one of rapid growth in the community pasture system of Saskatchewan. In this five-year period, a further 51 pastures totalling 643,729 acres were developed (Figure 10). The majority of these (39) were cooperative pastures of which 12 were in the vicinity of Manito Lake and Little Manito Lake. The new coopera-tive pastures averaged 5,660 acres. Although the Provincial pastures in this period increased by only five the new area committed to such pastures amounted to some 140,337 acres. This vast increase was due

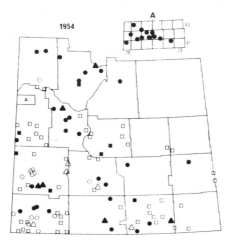

Figure 10.   Location of Community Pastures, 1954.

approximately equally to increase in the area of previous pastures
(with the exception of Matador), and new pastures, so that with the
exclusion of Matador (116,390 acres) the Provincial pastures now
averaged 15,000 acres.   The seven P.F.R.A. pastures established in
this period were all large but the two to the north of the old
P.F.R.A. boundary in C.D.'s 13 and 16 were 38,760 and 64,960 acres
respectively.

        The method of establishing cooperative pastures was clear
cut.   As land became available, incorporated cooperative livestock
associations requested the lease of such lands to establish pastures.
With a few exceptions these seldom exceeded 5,000 acres.   However,
the difference between provincial and P.F.R.A. assignments was less
clear.   Generally, but not always (depending largely upon title
problems) large pasture areas were developed by the Land Utilization Branch of the P.F.R.A.   Smaller areas or areas with difficult
land title were developed by the Provincial Department of Agriculture as Provincial community pastures.

        In the years since 1954 there has been a gradual expansion
northward and north-eastward in community pasture development in
Saskatchewan, with an increasing emphasis on Provincial and cooperative pastures (although P.F.R.A. initiated the development of a
series of community pastures in the various Indian Reserves of

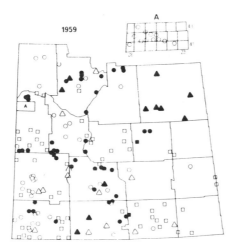

1959

Figure 11.   Location of Community Pastures, 1959.

eastern and northern Saskatchewan during the late 1960's).

    Between 1955 and 1959, 62 new pastures averaging only 2,900
acres were developed, of which 48 were cooperative pastures and
accounted for 140,281 acres. These were located mainly in the
western half of the Province (Figure 11) with one-fifth north of
the old P.F.R.A. boundary. The number of Provincial pastures
doubled in this period to 22, more than half of which were north
of the old P.F.R.A. boundary, mostly in the north-east of the
Province (Census Division 14). These averaged almost 9,900 acres
each and thus were notably smaller than those developed prior to
1955. Despite the lack of large areas suitable for P.R.F.A. pastures three new P.F.R.A. pastures averaged 37,400 acres and included more land than the 11 new Provincial pastures.

    This pattern of declining increase in pasture development
continued through the 1960-64 and 1965-69 periods, and there has
been greater emphasis on smaller pastures, both provincial and
P.F.R.A., and on the development of Provincial rather than P.F.R.A.
and cooperative pastures (Figures 12 and 13). Since the early
1960's much of the stimulus to develop small Provincial and cooperative pastures has come from the availability of ARDA (Agricultural and Regional Development Act) Funds. These have been
available for the Provincial Government to purchase and improve

139

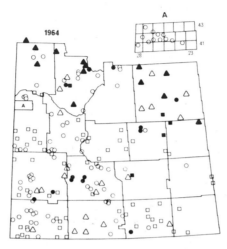

Figure 12. Location of Community Pastures, 1964.

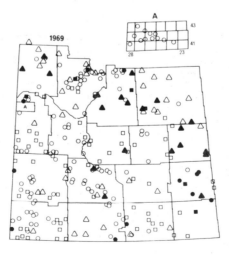

Figure 13. Location of Community Pastures, 1969.

140

land for community pastures (both Provincial and Cooperative).
ARDA funds here placed the Provincial Department of Agriculture on
a competitive footing with the P.F.R.A. in its ability to acquire
and develop pasture although the general rule of P.F.R.A. responsibility for the development of the largest pastures has remained.
In the late 1960's, the P.F.R.A. turned its attention to Indian
Reservations and in cooperation with Reservation Councils began the
development of community pastures for use by nearby livestock
owners. At the end of 1969 there were 67 P.F.R.A. community pastures which averaged 27,690 acres, 51 Provincial pastures which
averaged 12,130 acres and 124 cooperative pastures which averaged
4,670 acres.

CONCLUSION

The community pasture system of Saskatchewan represents an
obvious tool of land policy in that province. Since the late 1930's
some 3.05 million acres of land regarded as submarginal for arable
farming have been incorporated into these pastures. The initial development of this system appears to have been in response to a
perceived need to diversity farming activities in south-western
Saskatchewan. In the late 1930's, the basis for expansion of the
community pasture system appears to have changed to a need to rehabilitate eroded land resources, but again in the 1950's the importance of diversifying farming activities became the dominant reason
for their being. Throughout this period, community pastures have
represented one means of increasing both the area of farm land
available for certain farmers and the efficiency of farm labour.

Local environmental conditions have played a major role in
determining the distribution of community pastures since the 1930's
and this form of land use has provided an ideal means of sharing the
use of pockets of submarginal lands amongst farmers from surrounding
areas. Improvements in cultivation techniques, the introduction of
better pasture grasses and more widespread livestock farming have
perhaps reduced the necessity for use of submarginal agricultural
lands in this way. However, the ever-growing demand for new pastures and for livestock agistment in older pastures indicates that
a broad spectrum of the farming community benefits from the presence
of community pastures throughout the Province.

F.H. Auld, Deputy Minister for Agriculture in Saskatchewan
from 1917 to 1959 did not leave personal papers which might be used
to judge more clearly his role in the development of the community
pasture system. However, his Department of Agriculture files indicate his keen and continuing interest in the development of community
pastures, whether P.F.R.A., Provincial or cooperative, throughout
his official career. His early correspondence suggested a preference
for the cooperative organization, and he apparently resented the loss
of Saskatchewan Crown lands to the P.F.R.A. However, from 1921 to

1959 he was actively engaged in promoting the development of the Saskatchewan community pasture system.

The economic efficiency of community pastures and especially of the larger P.F.R.A. pastures has been called into question increasingly in the last decade, and the rate of pasture expansion even as small cooperative ventures appears to be slowing, although ARDA funds are still available for their construction. It therefore appears that the community pastures system of Saskatchewan is close to its peak of development and some major change in policy, especially with regard to the larger units, may be forthcoming in the next few years.

SOURCES

Annual Report, Saskatchewan Department of Agriculture, 1907.

Better Farming Conference (Regina: Government Printer Saskatchewan, 1920).

Report of the Royal Commission of Inquiry into Farming Conditions in the Province of Saskatchewan (Regina: Government Printer Saskatchewan, 1922).

Saskatchewan Department of Agriculture Files. Saskatchewan Archives. Regina Section.

Pierce, W.M. *The Matador Land and Cattle Company* (Norman: University of Oklahoma Press, 1964).

Deputy Minister of Agriculture Files. Saskatchewan Archives. Regina Section.

Land Utilization Board Files. Saskatchewan Archives, Regina Section.

Community Pastures Files. P.F.R.A., Regina.

THE AIYANSH VOLCANO

Vilho Wuorinen
University of Victoria

Although Canada's west coast forms part of the Pacific Rim of Fire, none of the world's more than five hundred active volcanoes are located in this country.[1] However, two inactive volcanoes, British Columbia's Mount Edziza and Aiyansh Volcano, have both erupted within the last 1,800 years. The Mount Edziza area was established as a provincial park in 1972; Aiyansh Volcano and its associated lava flow are expected to be incorporated into the parks system in the near future. As part of the provincial Parks Branch interpretive program, the author conducted a geomorphological study of the Aiyansh area in the summer of 1974.

The volcano is located at 55°07'N 128°54'W, on a small tributary of the Tseax River which in turn empties into the Nass (Figure 1). The Tseax-Kitsumkalum valley, stretching a hundred kilometres between the city of Terrace on the Skeena and the village of Aiyansh by the Nass, is thought to represent the surface expression of a major fault.[2] The hot springs at Lakelse Lake and Ansedagan Creek, as well as Aiyansh Volcano indicate the presence of a disturbed zone. Lava flowed down Crater Creek valley to the Tseax, and then to the Nass to form a thirty kilometre square lava plain on the south bank.

Aiyansh Volcano was formed some 200 to 300 years ago, making it the most recent volcanic eruption known in Canada. Indian legends place the event in about 1770, a date seemingly supported by dendrochronology. Trees said to have been cut in 1898 were found to have their barked stripped 128 years earlier.[3] Since the trees were cut at the place where local Indians had established their first refuge after being forced to evacuate their village as the lava advanced, it has been suggested that the trees were stripped to provide material for shelter. Radio-carbon dating of cottonwood killed by the flow has indicated an age of 220 years± 130 B.P.[4]

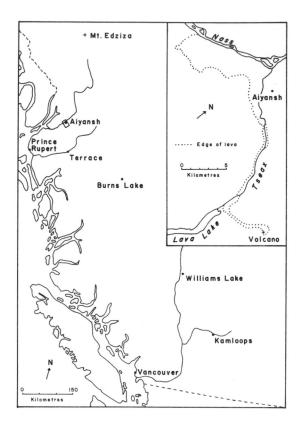

Figure 1. Location of Aiyansh Volcano

Several factors have operated to make this area unique in
Canada for the study of minor volcanic features (Figure 2). While
Mount Edziza has built an extensive lava plateau in a series of
eruptions spread over thousands of years, the Aiyansh lava flow is
the result of a single eruption. The location of the vent on the
side of a narrow valley with a steep gradient, allowing the lava to
escape readily, has prevented obliteration of the sub-surface be-
neath the lava. Representing only a single flow, the original vent
area can be determined with some certainty. Although general erosion
of the surface area is negligible, small streams flowing down the
valley sides have cut through the cinders, exposing near-vertical
cross sections of the tephra layers at regular intervals away from
the main cone. Due to its comparative youth, the area has not yet
been completely masked with vegetative growth.

Figure 2. Aiyansh Volcano, showing younger cone nested
in remains of older, larger cone. Concentric
collapse depressions can be seen around main
crater. Secondary cone is visible to north
of Lower Melita Lake (BC 443-047).

GEOMORPHOLOGY OF CONE AREA

The major structure in the vent area is a cinder cone nested
in the remains of an older, larger cone. This younger (main) cone
stands about 100 metres above the lava surface and contains a crater
estimated as being 80 metres in depth (Figure 3). The cinders on
both the inner and outer walls were measured at an angle of repose
of 35 degrees, but are so loosely packed that walking on the sides
is extremely difficult.

The rim of the main cone is encircled by a series of collapse
depressions in the form of rings, with the largest measuring 3 metres
in depth by 10 metres across (Figure 4). They result from the crater
walls slumping inward following the lowering of the magma level in
the conduit.

A large 30 metre high secondary cone, situated less than 600
metres to the north of the main cone, differs in that it has no
crater. This unusual feature results from a weakening in the strength
of the ejections from the throat of the vent toward the end of an

145

Figure 3.   Crater of main cone, 80 metres deep

Figure 4.   Collapse depression on rim of main cone.

eruption, allowing the centre to be filled with ejecta.[5]

    Several smaller cinder cones with spatter-welded fragments, found near the base of the main cone, represent an intermediate stage in the gradation from cinder cones to purely spatter cones consisting of congealed lava only. A decrease in the explosiveness of the eruoption, or an increase in the fludity of the magma, or both, will reduce the cinder content of a cone.[6]

    Compared to the jagged black surface of the larger cones, several small hornitos are a relief to the eye with their smooth red interior surfaces (Figure 5). Built up when spatter erupts through the surface of a pahoehoe flow, they are differentiated from other volcanic cones in that they derive their lava from within the flow rather than from a fissure or vent. They can only be found in the

Figure 5.   Interior of hornito, showing smooth congealed
            surface resulting from flowback of lava spurt.

147

immediate vicinity of the source of the flow, as the lava must still be very fluid and gas-charged in order to spurt out of small cracks in the crust of the flow.

In addition to the cinders and lava spatter which constitute the bulk of the material in the cones, volcanic bombs represent a small but interesting component. Found mainly on the east side of the main cone, they appear in a wide variety of sizes and shapes. Ejected as molten blobs of lava, they congeal into round, almond-shaped, ribbon-like, or spindle-shaped lumps before striking the ground (Figure 6). A larger type, the breadcrust bomb, has a netted pattern of open cracks attributable to stretching of the skin as a result of continued swelling of the gas-rich core after the external crust has formed.

Figure 6. Volcanic bomb. Knife is 18 cm. long.

A small stream has eroded the west face of the old cone, exposing the contact with the pre-eruption surface. An irregular till surface is separated from the cinders by a thin white ash layer which is intermingled with small quantities of incinerated bark and wood.

To the north and east of the main cone, streams have carved their way through the scoria, leaving almost vertical banks standing. Where slumping has occurred, charred remains of standing trees attest

to a speed of cinder accumulation so rapid that the bark on the
trees did not burn but was instead preserved as charcoal. Some
banding is evident in the tephra layers, probably from intermittent
ash falls (Figure 7). Further to the east, the cinders decrease
in thickness and particle size, but are still evident up to two
kilometres away.

Figure 7. Cinder accumulation to east of main cone.
Banding is probably due to intermittent ash
falls. Pole is one metre long.

Based on the highest elevation where solidified flow lava can
be seen, the main point of lava emission appears to be buried under
the northeast wall of the main cone. From here the lava flowed both
east and west as well as across the valley floor. Since the valley
has a sharp downward gradient to the west, most of the lava was

forced in this direction, but two tongues of lava crossed the valley, damming the stream to form Lower and Upper Melita Lakes.

Although the lava flow extends for over thirty kilometres, some flow features are only clearly visible in the first few hundred metres from the vent, where the lava was most liquid and gaseous. In addition to the hornitos previously described, lava moraines are another example of such features. The flow of a lava stream may be compared to that of a glacier, but its lateral moraines derive their material from a different source in each case. Congealed blocks are rafted on the surface of the lava stream, with some blocks falling over the edges of the raised flow. When the lava level recedes, the still fluid lava near the centre of the stream continues to flow out, leaving the raised sides.

With increasing distance from the vent, a crust forms over the flow surface. Underneath this crust, which is a poor conductor of heat, the liquid lava continues to flow at varying speeds, as dictated by local topography and relation to the centre of the flow. Slower moving parts receive less new heat and solidify, leaving only a few pipes in which the lava remains liquid and fully mobile. When the supply of lava is cut off at the source, the liquid drains away, leaving a hollow tube. One such lava tunnel near the main cone measures three metres in diameter and extends for thirty metres. It has a flat bottom and a rounded ceiling festooned with fragile lava stalactites. Ice found at the bottom of the tunnel in late July serves as a good indicator of the heat-insulating qualities of the congealed lava.

ERUPTION OF AIYANSH VOLCANO

Volcanic eruptions have traditionally been classified by designating them by the names of famous volcanoes which exemplify each characteristic type of activity (e.g., Hawaiian, Strombolian, Vulcanian). Bearing in mind that any one volcano usually exhibits a wider range of activity than is accounted for under any one classification, the Aiyansh eruption seems to resemble the Strombolian type most closely. Emission of moderately fluid lava is accompanied by weak to violent ejection of pasty fluid blobs. Cinder cones are built around vents from the ejection of volcanic bombs, cinder, and small amounts of ash.[7]

From the depositional evidence at the site and by analogy with the recorded events at the birth of another Strombolian type volcano, Paricutin,[8] it is possible to attempt a reconstruction of the sequence of events during the eruption of Aiyansh Volcano with some certainty. Violent local earth tremors precede the initial perforation. The ground swells, and cracks appear at the top of the mound. Escaping volcanic gas pushes out earth, steam, and red-hot stones, followed by ash and cinders in ever-increasing quantities.

Of this initial train of deposits, only the ash and cinder have been identified, the other ejecta presumably being buried under the main cone.

The pattern of cinder accumulation around the cone indicates that the main conduit was inclined slightly to the southeast. It is unlikely that an up-valley (west) wind alone could be responsible for the lack of tephra to the west of the cone, although it probably was a contributing factor in spreading the finer particles so far to the east.

Lava issuing from the base of the cone forms a dam across the valley, and the accumulation of water combined with magmatic gases leads to intermittent explosions which are interspersed with lava fountaining in the crater. Perhaps it is such a phreatic explosion which finally shatters the main cone, disrupting the main conduit. Circular pits in the cinder surface, some reaching a depth of one metre, are located several hundred metres to the east of the old cone. They may have originated when giant volcanic bombs were hurled out in this terminal explosion.

A new cinder cone begins to form within the remains of the original, but the ejections are now so weak that very little tephra is deposited beyond the cone walls. Magma rising and subsiding in the new conduit is accompanied by inward slumping of the crater walls. As a result of the disrupted conduits, small secondary cones are formed. The fact that none of these cones has well-defined craters indicates their birth when magmatic pressures were waning. Within a few days or weeks, all activity ceases.

CONCLUSION

The need for preservation of this unique corner of British Columbia has been recognized in the plans to establish the area as a class "A" park.[9] Designation of the site as a provincial park, coupled with increasing traffic on the Terrace-Stewart-Cassiar highway, can be expected to result in an influx of tourists to the area. Parks Branch decision makers will then be faced with the problem of reconciling greater public access with the necessity to preserve the natural surface from the impact of such increased use.

The immediate volcano area represents the most fragile surface in the proposed park. Elsewhere, only the delicate vegetation would be seriously threatened by human feet, but each step on the steep cinder cone walls precipitates a minor slide. The main cone has already been marred by climbers using diverse paths in scaling its sides, and it has escaped major damage only because the site can now be reached only after a strenuous two-hour hike over jagged lava.

Further deterioration on and around the cone could be checked by establishing the Crater Creek portion of the park as a nature conservancy area,[10] thus preventing access roads from being built. An improved trail built over and beside the lava flow would become the only route to the site. Clearly marked self-guiding trails in the cone area, including a plant staircase up the main cone on a side hidden from general view, would discourage visitors from indiscriminate wandering over the fragile cinder surfaces.

Parks can serve many purposes within the overall one of recreation of the public, but each individual park offers attributes which must be considered in planning park use. In the case of Aiyansh Volcano, it is suggested that the main attraction is its scientific interest, a place of quiet where one can contemplate the awesome forces of nature. As such, it deserves to be maintained in its pristine state for future generations to enjoy.

ACKNOWLEDGMENTS

Field work for this paper was conducted while employed by the British Columbia Parks Branch which has kindly granted permission to use the material. Opinions expressed are those of the author, and do not necessarily reflect official policy of the Parks Branch.

SOURCES

[1] The criterion used here to identify a volcano as active is that it has erupted during recorded historic times. See Gordon A. Macdonald, *Volcanoes* (Englewood Cliffs, New Jersey: Prentice-Hall, Inc., 1972), 429-450.

[2] S. Duffell and J.G. Souther, *Geology of Terrace Map-Area, Memoir 329* (Ottawa: Geological Survey of Canada, 1964), 11.

[3] J.B. McCullagh, *Ignis, a Parable of the Great Lava Plain* (Aiyansh, B.C., 1918).

[4] A. Sutherland Brown, "Aiyansh lava flow, British Columbia," *Canadian Journal of Earth Sciences* 6, (1969), 1467.

[5] Macdonald, *op. cit.*, 185.   [6] Macdonald, *op. cit.*, 188.

[7] Macdonald, *op. cit.*, 211.

[8] Fred M. Bullard, *Volcanoes in History, in Theory, in Eruption* (Austin: University of Texas Press, 1962), 272-290.

[9] Class "A" parks are so designated in order to preserve outstanding natural features, and no other resourse use is permitted within their boundaries as is the case with class "B" parks. In 1973 there were 220 class "A" parks and 8 class "B" parks in B.C.

[10] Nature conservancy areas are zones within parks where construction of facilities other than trails is not permitted.

REFLECTION, HEATING, AND LONGWAVE EXCHANGE COEFFICIENTS FOR A DWARF APPLE ORCHARD

P.W. Suckling
The University of British Columbia

Radiation exchange above a canopy extends important controls on energy exchange within. Both determine the microclimate of the plant community and the important physiological processes of photosynthesis and transpiration. Although radiation exchanges of many crops have been studied (Monteith and Szeicz, 1961; Stanhill, Hofstede and Kalma, 1966; Idso, Baker and Blad, 1969; Impens and Lemeur, 1969; Davies and Buttimor, 1969), orchard crops have received little attention. The only studies known to the author are those by Kalma and Stanhill (1969) for an orange orchard in Israel and by Landsberg, Powell and Butler (1973) for an apple orchard in southern England.

Results from a study of the radiation balance of a single apple tree have been presented earlier (Proctor, Kyle and Davies, 1972). In this paper, the study is extended to a dwarf apple orchard.

RADIATION BALANCE RELATIONSHIPS

The radiation balance of a surface can be expressed as

$$Q^* = K^* + L^* \tag{1}$$

where Q^* is net radiation, K^* is net global radiation, L^* is net terrestrial or longwave radiation and $K^* = K\!\downarrow - K\!\uparrow = (1-\alpha)K\!\downarrow$ in which $\alpha = K\!\uparrow / K\!\downarrow$ is the surface reflection coefficient and $K\!\downarrow$ and $K\!\uparrow$ are the incoming and reflected components respectively. Routine measurements of Q^* are rare. To determine Q^* without direct measurements, the determination of bulk coefficients for the radiative behaviour of a surface is required. Presumably, these can be used to understand and model surface radiation behaviour. To date, this has not been successful.

Davies (1967) has related Q* and K↓ linearly as

$$Q* = a + bK\downarrow. \tag{2}$$

Having found values for a and b, he concluded that this relationship may be useful as a first approximation to determine net radiation for evaporation estimates.

Incorporating surface reflection, Monteith and Szeicz (1961) related Q* and K* as

$$Q* = a + bK*. \tag{3}$$

They defined a heating coefficient β= (1-b)/b, which allows equation 3 to become

$$Q* = L*(0) + K*/(1+\beta). \tag{4}$$

where L*(0) is net terrestrial radiation at K*=0. Derivation and further discussion of these concepts is given by Proctor *et al.*, (1972).

Gay (1971) observed that the statistical relationship between Q* and K* is difficult to justify. Combining equations 1 and 3,

$$K* + L* = a + bK*. \tag{5}$$

Here, K* appears on both sides of the equation. This accounts for high correlations between Q* and K*. Subtracting K* from both sides of equation 5,

$$L* = a + bK* - K* = a + (b-1)K*. \tag{6}$$

Therefore,

$$L* = L*(0) + \lambda K*. \tag{7}$$

Gay defined λ as a longwave exchange coefficient obtained directly from the regression of L* upon K*.

If either β or λ can be specified, Q* would then require only a measure of K* or its component K↓ if the reflection coefficient for the surface is known.

METHODS

This study was conducted at the Horticultural Experiment Station near Simcoe, Ontario (42°51' N, 80°16' W) during the summer of 1973. An orchard of *Malus pumila* Mill. cultivar Idared, on the clonal apple rootstock MM.106 was used. The trees were arranged in 5 rows of 15 trees each, with both trees and rows spaced 1.5 m apart. The trees were approximately 2 m tall in mid-June and had reached a height of 2.5 m by August. Measurements were obtained for half-hourly periods on six "bright" days (days with cloud cover less than 6/10) and five cloudy days.

Incoming global radiation was measured using a precision Eppley Model 2 pyranometer (Eppley Lab. Inc., Newport, R.I., U.S.A.). Reflected global radiation was obtained using a Kipp pyranometer (Kipp and Zonen, Delft, The Netherlands) mounted in an inverted position on a mast in the orchard at a height of about 0.5 m above the tops of the trees, resulting in a view factor of about 0.96 (Latimer, 1972). Mean daily reflection coefficients were calculated as the ratio of the daily totals of K↑ and K↓. This method avoids the biased weighting by daily extremity values that occurs when the daily mean of half-hourly reflection coefficient values is evaluated.

A net radiometer (Model S1, Swissteco Pty. Ltd., Melbourne, Australia) mounted on the same mast as the inverted pyranometer was used to measure net radiation.

RESULTS AND DISCUSSION

1. *Reflection Coefficient*

A distinct depencence of α on solar zenith angle was found on cloudy days (Figure 1). This confirms the results Proctor *et al.*, (1972) obtained for a single apple tree for bright days, and agrees with the results of numerous other workers (Monteith and Szeicz, 1961; Davics and Buttimor, 1969; Impens and Lemeur, 1969; Kyle, 1971).

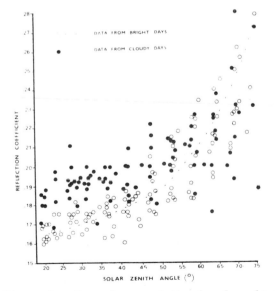

Figure 1.   Dependence of the dwarf apple orchard reflection coefficient on solar zenith angle.

Mean daily reflection coefficients were larger on cloudy days (Table 1). Pooling all data, overall mean reflection coefficient were 0.178 for bright days and 0.192 for cloudy days. These results agree favourably with those of Kalma and Stanhill (1969) for an orange orchard (0.16), of Landsberg *et al.*, (1973) for an apple orchard (0.13 to 0.19), and of Proctor *et al.*, (1972) for an apple tree (0.162). Thus, dwarf and regular orchards have similar reflection coefficients.

TABLE 1

Reflection Coefficients and Regression Analyses

Date	Sky Condition	α	Q* upon K↓			Q* upon K*			L* upon K*				
			a	b	r	a	b	r	β	a	b	r	λ
Jun 19	cloudy	0.191	+ 2	.65	.991	+10	.78	.985	.285	+10	-.22	.853	-.22
Jun 25	bright	0.178	-46	.69	.997	-17	.79	.997	.269	-17	-.21	.959	-.21
Jun 26	cloudy	0.190	-12	.69	.995	- 4	.84	.994	.203	- 4	-.17	.876	-.17
Jul 9	bright	0.175	-33	.65	.998	- 6	.74	.996	.348	- 6	-.26	.972	-.26
Jul 23	bright	0.183	-47	.69	.997	-27	.80	.997	.244	-27	-.20	.949	-.20
Aug 7	cloudy	0.196	-45	.73	.994	-33	.89	.994	.125	-33	-.11	.737	-.11
Aug 12	bright	0.179	-60	.74	.99	-38	.87	.995	.149	-38	-.13	.908	-.13
Aug 14	cloudy	0.190	-36	.75	.995	-29	.90	.993	.112	-29	-.10	.673	-.10
Aug 15	bright	0.179	-42	.71	.997	-33	.85	.996	.183	-33	-.16	.909	-.16
Aug 27	cloudy	0.185	+ 6	.63	.988	+ 7	.78	.990	.284	+ 7	-.22	.891	-.22
Sept 4	bright	0.172	-36	.73	.992	-20	.85	.992	.175	-20	-.15	.891	-.15
Pooled data			-14	.66	.992	- 4	.786	.992	.272	- 4	-.214	.901	-.214

Legend: α = reflection coefficient;
         a = intercept;
         b = regression coefficient;
         r = correlation coefficient;
         β and λ = heating and longwave exchange coefficients

2. *Regressions of Radiation Balance Components*

Linear correlations were obtained between Q* and K↓, Q* and K*, and L* and K* (Table 1). For the first regression, correlation coefficients exceeded 0.99 on all days. Values of the intercept *a* ranged from +6 to -60 Wm^{-2} with a pooled value of -14 Wm^{-2} while the regression coefficient *b* ranged from 0.63 to 0.75 with a pooled value of 0.66. This regression coefficient was higher than the 0.617 reported by Davies (1967).

For the regression of Q* and K*, correlation coefficients exceeded 0.985 on all days. Heating coefficients ranged between 0.112 and 0.348 with a pooled value of 0.272 and displayed no apparent

dependence on sky conditions. Landsberg *et al.*, (1973) obtained β
values for an apple orchard ranging from 0.2 to 0.6 with an average
of 0.305. Results for a single tree (Proctor *et al.*, 1972) ranged
from 0.101 to 0.380 under bright skies with a pooled mean of 0.165.
The mean of the present results differs by 0.03 and 0.11 from these
two studies respectively. The significance of these differences
(dβ) to Q* estimation was analyzed. Differentiating equation 4,

$$\frac{dQ*}{Q*} = \frac{-d\beta}{1+\beta} \left[1 + \frac{L*(0)}{K*} (1+\beta) \right]^{-1}. \qquad (8)$$

For dβ = 0.03 and 0.11, dQ*/Q* was found for β ranging from 0.06 to
0.39 and L*(0)/K* ranging from −0.15 to 0.03, which includes the
range of values found in this study (Table 2). From the table, the
differences between the mean β value in the present study and those
reported in the other two studies result in 2-3% and 7-12% differences in Q* estimation respectively. Since Q* cannot be measured to
an accuracy better than about 10% (Latimer, 1972), these mean seasonal β differences are not significant. However, to calculate Q*
on a daily basis, the wide range of β values found in each study pro-
hibits the use of a single β value for an apple orchard since much
greater errors in Q* estimation would occur.

Correlation coefficients for the L* and K* regression were
not so high (Table 1). Values of λ ranged from −0.100 to −0.258
with a mean of −0.214 and showed no detectable difference between
bright and cloudy days. Proctor *et al.*, (1972) report a similar
range of λ between −0.090 and −0.276 with a mean of −0.142. The
differences between the two mean λ values is 0.07. The significance
of this difference (dλ) to L* estimation was analyzed. Equation 7
can be differentiated to

$$\frac{dL*}{L*} = d\lambda \left[\lambda + \frac{L*(0)}{K*} \right]^{-1}. \qquad (9)$$

For dλ = 0.07, dL*/L* was found for λ to range from −0.30 to −0.09;
a range of L*(0)/K* is the same as the heating coefficient analysis
(Table 3). Differences in L* estimation of 16 to 233% were found.
Hence, small variations in λ produce significant differences in
estimation of L* for the mean seasonal values. The importance of
this error may, however, be small in Q* estimations since K* is
usually the dominant term in equation 1. Again the wide range of
values found prohibited the use of a single λ value for daily Q*
estimations.

CONCLUSIONS

The reflection coefficient results found for a single tree
by Proctor *et al.*, (1972) can be applied to a complete apple orchard.
Dependence of α on solar zenith angle has been confirmed.

TABLE 2

Values of dQ*/Q* as Effected by Heating
Coefficient Differences

(a) dβ = 0.03

L*(0)/K*

β	-0.15	-0.12	-0.09	-0.06	-0.03	0.00	+0.03
0.06	.034	.032	.031	.030	.029	.028	.027
0.09	.033	.032	.031	.029	.028	.028	.027
0.12	.032	.031	.030	.029	.028	.027	.026
0.15	.032	.030	.029	.028	.027	.026	.025
0.18	.031	.030	.028	.027	.026	.025	.025
0.21	.030	.029	.028	.027	.026	.025	.024
0.24	.030	.028	.027	.026	.025	.024	.023
0.27	.029	.028	.027	.026	.025	.024	.023
0.30	.029	.027	.026	.025	.024	.023	.022
0.33	.028	.027	.026	.025	.023	.023	.022
0.36	.028	.026	.025	.024	.023	.022	.021
0.39	.027	.026	.025	.024	.023	.022	.021

(b) dβ = 0.11

L*(0)/K*

β	-0.15	-0.12	-0.09	-0.06	-0.03	0.00	+0.03
0.06	.123	.119	.115	.111	.107	.104	.101
0.09	.121	.116	.112	.108	.104	.101	.098
0.12	.118	.113	.109	.105	.102	.098	.095
0.15	.116	.111	.107	.103	.099	.096	.092
0.18	.113	.109	.104	.100	.097	.093	.090
0.21	.111	.106	.102	.098	.094	.091	.088
0.24	.109	.104	.100	.096	.092	.089	.086
0.27	.107	.102	.098	.094	.090	.087	.083
0.30	.105	.100	.096	.092	.088	.085	.081
0.33	.103	.098	.094	.090	.086	.083	.080
0.36	.102	.096	.092	.088	.084	.081	.078
0.39	.100	.095	.090	.086	.083	.079	.076

TABLE 3

Values of dL*/L* as Effected by Longwave
Exchange Coefficient Differences

$d\lambda = 0.07$

	L*(0)/K*						
λ	-0.15	-0.12	-0.09	-0.06	-0.03	0.00	+0.03
-0.30	.156	.167	.179	.194	.212	.233	.259
-0.27	.167	.179	.194	.212	.233	.259	.292
-0.24	.179	.194	.212	.233	.259	.292	.333
-0.21	.194	.212	.233	.259	.292	.333	.389
-0.18	.212	.233	.259	.292	.333	.389	.467
-0.15	.233	.259	.292	.333	.389	.467	.583
-0.12	.259	.292	.333	.389	.467	.583	.778
-0.09	.292	.333	.389	.467	.583	.778	1.17
-0.06	.333	.389	.467	.583	.778	1.17	2.33

Analysis of heating and longwave exchange coefficients yields results similar to other studies. However, the present analysis has shown that, while defining a single value of β and possibly λ for an orchard may be useful on a seasonal basis, it cannot be used to estimate Q* for shorter time periods. In attempts to attain Q* for short-term estimates, an alternate modelling approach is, therefore, recommended. This could include the use of meteorological measurements and models for each of the terms in the radiation balance.

ACKNOWLEDGMENTS

I wish to thank Dr. J.A. Davies of McMaster University for his guidance and supervision throughout this study. Dr. J.T.A. Proctor and the staff of the Horticultural Experiment Station provided considerable assistance. This study was supported, in part, by the National Research Council of Canada.

REFERENCES

Davies, J.A. "A note on the relationship between net radiation and solar radiation," *Quart. J. R. Met. Soc.*, 93, (1967), 109-115.

Davies, J.A. and P.H. Buttimor. "Reflection coefficients, heating coefficients and net radiation at Sim coe, southern Ontario," *Agric. Meteor.*, 6, (1969), 373-386.

Gay, L.W. "The regression of net radiation upon solar radiation," *Arch. Meteor. Geophys. Bioklim.*, Series B, 19, (1971).

Idso, S.B., D.G. Baker and B.L. Blad. "Relations of radiation fluxes over natural surfaces," *Quart. J. R. Met. Soc.*, 95, (1969), 244-257.

Impens, I.I. and R. Lemeur. "The radiation balance of several field crops," *Arch. Meteor. Gophys. Bioklim.*, Series B, 17, (1969), 261–268.

Kalma, J.D. and G. Stanhill. "The radiation climate of an irrigated orange plantation," *Sol. Energy*, 12, (1969), 491–508.

Kyle, W.J. *Daytime Radiation Regimes Within a Corn Canopy* (Hamilton: Publications Climatology No. 2, McMaster University, 1971), 140 p.

Landsberg, J.J., D.B.B. Powell and D.R. Butler. "Microclimate in an apple orchard," *J. Appl. Ecol.*, 10, (1973), 881–896.

Latimer, J.R. *Radiation Measurement* (Ottawa: Int. Field Year Great Lakes/ Int. Hydrol. Decade Technical Manual Series No. 2, (1972), 53 p.

Monteith, J.L. and G. Szeicz. "The radiation balance of bare soil and vegetation," *Quart. J.R. Met. Soc.*, 87, (1961), 159–170.

Proctor, J.T.A., W.J. Kyle and J.A. Davies. "The radiation balance of an apple tree," *Can. J. Bot.*, 50, (1972), 1731–1740.

Stanhill, G., G.J. Hofstede and J.D. Kalma. "Radiation balance of natural and agricultural vegetation," *Quart. J. R. Met. Soc.*, 92, (1966), 128–140.

ABSTRACTS

ABSTRACTS OF PAPERS PRESENTED at the annual meeting of the
Western Division of the Canadian Association of Geographers, Van-
couver City College, Langara Campus, Vancouver, British Columbia,
March, 1975, but not printed in this volume.

R. Baldwin and M.C. Brown:

A GENERAL THEORETICAL MODEL OF AIR FLOW
IN CAVE AND MINES

Cave systems with two or more entrances at different eleva-
tions often exhibit seasonally directional air flow. This is a
thermally induced flow analogous to the movement of air in a chimney
and is referred to as the "chimney" or "stack" effect. Previous
attempts to model cave winds of this type have greatly simplified
the phenomenon by assuming *static* conditions and then estimating air
density differences between the cave atmosphere and the outside air.
This approach is basically incorrect when applied to dynamic conditions, and may lead to substantial errors in estimating speleomicro-
climatic parameters. Wigley and Brown (1972, Boundary Layer Meteorology) have modelled temperature and humidity distributions in such
caves under dynamic conditions by applying the fundamentals of heat
and mass transfer. This paper summarizes an attempt to model air
velocity distribution by extending their results to include other
parameters. The cave or mine is considered a semi-infinite, wet-
walled cylinder, and the principles of the thermodynamics of com-
pressible fluid flow are applied. The results are of significance
to geomorphologists investigating inaccessible karst systems, bio-
speleologists concerned with the distribution of life in caves, and
mine ventilation engineers.

R. Blencoe:

GEOGRAPHY AND PUBLIC PARTICIPATION: A HUMANISTIC APPROACH

Contemporary public participation in the decision making
process is viewed by some as a social revolution. Academics and

progressive decision makers alike offer gestures of good will to
theories of citizen involvement. The more radical elements theorize
upon its potential as a revolutionary or evolutionary force within
society. This is indeed highly speculative, if not slightly naive.
As it exists now, it is used as a panacea to the increasing subjuga-
tion of the individual by remote, highly centralized bureaucracies.
Rather than be limited to this co-option, geography should be an
extension of thinking beyond reform, beyond an elite public participation. True revolutionary dialogue would encourage the abandon-
ment of our desire for the collectivisation of society and population aggregates, and replace them with communities, and individuals.

T.R. Boss:

VEGETATION STUDY OF A POWERLINE RIGHT-OF-WAY, WHATCOM COUNTY, WASHINGTON

The vegetation along a 25 kilometer segment of the Bonne-
ville Power Administration Powerline Right-of-way was studied in
relation to human activity, altitude, slope, aspect, and the regional
vegetation. Nine study sites were located within this 25 Km segment,
with four, 50 meter, quadrant transects strung at each site to
obtain frequency and cover values. Two transects were laid near the
edges of the right-of-way, one in the center of the right-of-way,
and one transect along the major trodden throughfare within the
particular site.

A cluster analysis of the nine sites, based on the floristic
data, was computed and three groups were formed.

Preliminary conclusions were that definite species and life
forms occupied different "areas" of the right-of-way, both on an
intra- and intersite basis.

D. Gill:

KINETIC ENERGY AS A CLIMATIC PROCESS ALONG NORTHERN FLOODPLAINS AND DELTAS

Along north-flowing rivers, spring breakup represents a
significant transfer of kinetic energy from headwater areas to their
floodplains and deltas within a short period of time. To illustrate
this, the Mackenzie Delta has the highest summer temperatures of any
location on the North American continent at that latitude (68° to
69°N), and the spring flood is one of the principal processes of
this ameliorated climate. During mid-May, water under hydrostatic
pressure initiated by snowmelt runoff in the southwest portion of
the Mackenzie Basin begins to break through the Delta ice deck to
flood the snow-covered surfaces of distributaries, lakes, and their
shorelines. As breakup progresses, rapidly rising water causes the
channel and lake ice to lift and break through buoyancy release;

this broken ice is then flushed seaward, leaving open water in its place. At this time of year, water surfaces in the Mackenzie Delta absorb up to five times more solar radiation than the amount absorbed by a snow cover. Since some 50 per cent of the 6500 Km^2 surface of the Delta is covered by lakes and channels, it follows that the rapid change in the albedo of this surface, caused by overflow and "ice flushing," is highly significant to the Delta's heat budget. Greatly increased absorption of solar energy during and immediately following breakup enables air and water temperatures in the Delta to rise sooner and more rapidly than in adjacent tundra uplands. For example, at 1510 hours on 20 June 1973, the air temperature in the north central Mackenzie Delta was 19.5°C and the water was 16.0°C. By contrast, at Yaya Lake, located on Richards Island only 5 km northeast of the Delta, the air temperature at 1535 hours that day was 7.0°C; the lake was still mostly ice-covered, and water temperatures in small leads ranged from 0.0°C to 0.5°C. The ameliorated spring climate of the Mackenzie Delta greatly affects the phenology of plants growing there. For example, the feltleaf willow (*Salix alaxensis*), one of the most common shrubs of this region, experiences bud-burst two to three weeks earlier in the Delta than in nearby locations. In 1966 and 1967, bud-burst in the Delta was complete by the last week of May, whereas in the tundra uplands immediately adjacent to the east side of the Delta, bud-burst in the same species did not begin until the second week of June. Leaf elongation also exhibits marked contrast in growth rates between the Delta and adjacent areas: at Yaya Lake, the mean length of *Salix alaxensis* leaves (n=100) was 1.5 cm on 20 June 1973, while in the north-central portion of the Delta on that date, leaves from the same species (n=100) averaged 5.5 cm in length.

J.E. Hay:

CLIMATIC CHANGE: REVIEW AND PREVIEW

This paper examines the changes in such meteorological variables as temperature, precipitation, sunshine hours and storm day frequency for the Vancouver area over the last 50 years. The observed variations are discussed in the context of climatic fluctuations on larger time (geologic) and space (hemispheric) scales. Following a brief examination of the current theories of climatic change the paper considers the likely variations in temperature conditions over the next 100 years.

C.C. Irby:

CONFLICT RESOLUTION AT AMBER VALLEY, ALBERTA

This paper addresses the subject of conflict resolution in a rural Alberta community. [Even though all persons in the community "grew up in the shadows of the Church," and there are elements of Christian fervor and principles among the people, its role as a social organizing agent has been minor. Consequently, the role of the Church is of minor importance in the resolution of the conflict.] The major community conflicts arose as a result of disappearing social institutions, namely, the school and the post office.

Amber Valley, like more than 5,000 other rural communities throughout the Province, lost its post office in the mid-1960's. As a major social institution in the community where ideas were exchanged (i.e., gossip), its demise effectively ended the community's reliable internal communications link.

The loss of the primary social institution, the school—life-blood of the community—occurred in the 1950's. It was the loss of the school that precipitated the great conflict which revolved around the question of education for the community's children. After the school was closed, parents were neither in control nor in agreement with the kind of education their children were receiving. As a result of the distances they had to travel to get to and from school, community contact and supervision of the children decreased —creating friction within and between families. Some families opted out by moving to urban centres to face different conflicts. This paper is about those parents and children who remained to tell the story.

A. MacPherson and R.A. Phillips:

LANDSCAPE EVALUATION: THE POSSIBILITY OF CRITICISM

Critical evaluation of place has intermittently attracted the attention of geographers, and interest appears to be increasing. A paper on the subject was read at the 1971 meeting of the Division, and a recent resource paper on visual blight drew attention to the need for criticism in a humane geography. Many students may believe that environmental quality can, in many situations, be no more than a matter of opinion, or else that the questions raised are too difficult for immediate attention. Geographers should be the best-informed and most disinterested critics of place, but they tend to leave questions of quality to the prejudices, tastes, and special interests of others.

According to their particular professional interests, geographers study, describe, and explain much as do critics of the arts; but unlike conventional critics they hesitate qualitatively to evaluate the places they seek to understand. This paper discusses aspects of geographical applications of criticism. Problems arise from the many ways of looking at places and from the varying extent to which these may be interpreted for "meaning"; also place, as an artifact, tends to be evaluated by criteria apart from its strict content and immediate function. While geography straddles the

natural sciences, the social sciences, and the humanities, the fabric
of the discipline is far from a seamless web; geographers strive
to study and explain landscapes "scientifically," but evaluation of
these demands other kinds of criteria.

C. Murray:
BONAPARTE-LAC DU BOIS MORATORIUM (KAMLOOPS AREA)

The concept of multiple-use, while well understood, has too
often been ineffectual in practice. A fact of considerable importance in this regard is the sing-factor approach to the management
of land and resources. The industry or government department concerned is responsible for utilizing the area around its particular
("prime") resource; other uses (where they are in fact considered)
are of secondary importance.

In Kamloops recently a group of citizens prevailed upon the
Hon. Robert Williams (Lands, Forests, & Water Resources) to issue a
one-year moratorium on development in the Bonaparte Plateau area
north of the city while a committee comprising local departmental
heads undertook a study of the "wilderness core" and adjacent forest
and range land with a view to developing an integrated-use policy
for the area.

The rapid population growth, an affluent community (with
much motorized recreation), and the activities of local lumber com-
panies have placed increasing pressures on the areas surrounding
Kamloops. This, coupled with the fragile nature of the semi-arid
grazing lands and upland meadows and forests, led to the concern
shown by the citizens' group, and a year's study culminated in the
presentation of the brief six months ago, and the Minister's pre-
Christmas decision.

The matter is not yet resolved (the study is barely under
way), but the appointment of the local departmental heads to the
committee, under the chairmanship of the forestry department was
not entirely to the satisfaction of the group presenting the brief.
It would appear difficult for traditional attitudes not to intrude
in the committee's deliberations. The appointment of someone well-
qualified in natural-resource management and free of the limitations
of representing a vested departmental interest would have been more
desirable.

More information on the progress of this study should be
available in early March at the time of the conference at Langara.

W.L. Mykes:

FACTORS IN RESISTANCE TO ANNEXATION

A number of problems arise from the fact that the "functional area" of a city expands beyond the de jure region. The population spills over the urban boundaries to suburbs, smaller towns, and rural areas but remains effectively linked to the central city. Because this population is beyond its jurisdiction, the urban administration cannot control development in these sectors. When attempts at control are undertaken, particularly if this takes the form of annexation, strong resistance tends to occur.

The objective is to find out who resists, where and why this resistance occurs, what the dominant factors in resistance are, and how it can be predicted. The problem in general is a dynamic one; there are spatial change processes at work which in turn may generate a resistance process. Accordingly, spatial change processes are briefly examined. These changes create a lag in which the de jure and de facto regions become maladjusted resulting in a stress situation. There are various political spatial solutions to the problem, some potentially more acceptable than others to the populace.

Resistance behaviour is examined in general. Various types and sources of resistance, and levels of effectiveness, are identified. Potential sources of explanation for resistance are discussed.

The specific focus is on resistance attitudes to annexation expressed by outlying urban communities toward an expanding city. A resistance process framework is presented as a preliminary explanation of resistance behaviour, and as an organizing device for the examination of selected resistance hypotheses. It is intended that these hypotheses will be tested in St. Albert, a community that would be annexed if Edmonton's planning proposals were carried out.

T.R. Oke and T. Brown:

EDDY CORRELATION MEASUREMENTS OF SENSIBLE HEAT FLUXES IN RURAL AND URBAN ENVIRONMENTS

The eddy correlation approach to the measurement of turbulent fluxes is reviewed, and the theory and construction of the relatively simple yaw sphere-thermometer system (YST) which employs this method in the measurement of sensible heat fluxes is outlined and illustrated.

Field experience gained in the use of the YST system over a four-year period, and in a range of rural and urban situations in British Columbia is evaluated. Results are presented from experiments conducted near the surface of long grass at Ladner, of dry alfalfa at Kamloops, of dry of dry scrub at White Lake, of a roof in Vancouver, and at 50 m on a tower in Burnaby. The sensible heat flux results are discussed in the context of the complete energy balance by including concurrent net radiation and subsurface flux data. In particular the pioneering urban heat flux results are examined.

L. Skoda:

GEORGIA STRAIT URBAN REGION--A CARTOGRAPHIC PRESENTATION

The Census Metropolitan Areas of Vancouver and Victoria have been traditionally viewed as separate urban entities divided by the Strait of Georgia. More recently, they have been regarded as functionally part of a large coastal urban community identified as the Georgia Strait Urban Region.

This paper introduces a map of the Georgia Strait Urban Region which was prepared in response to shared interests and concerns with urbanization and land by the Ministry of State for Urban Affairs and Lands Directorate, Department of the Environment. The project was carried out under joint contract by the School of Community and Regional Planning, University of British Columbia and Canadian Cartographics Ltd., Coquitlam, British Columbia.

The map, which can best be described as "one page atlas," presents selected information on the extent of urbanization in the region and highlights some of the emerging trends, pressures and conflicts of the urbanization processes and their effect on the region's land resources. People, land and movement form the core topics around which the map information is organized providing background summaries to a number of issues of current public concern.

The project is in the final stages and it is hoped that printed copies of the map will be available for distribution to participants.

C.C. Smart:

SOME MORPHOLOGIC IMPLICATIONS OF THE
PROBABILITY TRANSITION MATRIX

A discrete time or space series can be transformed into positive and negative states. The transformation employed filters the information in various ways. Deviation from the mean produces a series with no statistical difference from the original. Deviation of a value from a preceding value filters low frequency components and change in deviation values are a yet higher order filter. High frequency elements may be filtered by lengthening the sampling interval or smoothing the series. Once the series is decomposed into the positive and negative states it may be represented by the probability transition matrix. The matrix describes the probability of

changing from, or remaining in, a particular state. It takes the
form

$$P_{ij} = \begin{matrix} P_{++} & P_{+-} \\ P_{-+} & P_{--} \end{matrix}$$

Where P++ and P-- represent residence in a particular state and
constitute the positive correlation diagonal. P+- and P-+ represent
the probabilities of changing state and are the anticorrelation diagonal. A dominant positive correlation diagonal represents a high
wavelength/leg length ratio and a dominant anticorrelation matrix a
lower ratio. A comparison of P++ and P-- describes any preference
for the components of a series to remain in a given state. If the
discrete series is in the space domain, then the matrix contains
morphologic information concerning the pattern of the series. The
technique was applied to meandering cave passages. An analysis of
the positive and anticorrelation diagonals describes the sensitivity
of the unit leg length to the smallest wavelength of the series.
The "symmetry" test compares P++ and P-- with their mean. This test
applied to the deviation from mean transformation describes any
directional preference in orientation. When applied to the first
order difference transform, the test describes differences in radius
of left and right curves. When applied to the second order difference transform it gives differences in the rate of inflection of
left and right curves. The nature of constraints on meander symmetry is unclear. Gross bedrock structure does not directly influence the cave meanders studied. The asymmetry under a given transform is independent of results under other transforms. The probability transition matrix is a sensitive descriptor of a series in
the time or space domain.

P. Stobie:

THE PROCESS OF PRIVATE REDEVELOPMENT IN KITSILANO

Geographical research concerning the private redevelopment
of the inner city in Canada has been almost totally morphological
in nature. (See for example, the work of Bourne and some of his
students at the University of Toronto). Yet, quite possibly the
most salient aspect of this process is the interplay of the involved
actors: the details of their decision making and the meeting of their
conflicting values about the urban landscape. For it is the results
of this exchange which, in large measure, determine the emerging
morphology of the inner city.

It is with just such a commutation still unfolding in Kitsilano, an inner city community in Vancouver, that this paper is
concerned. The involved actors are the staff and citizen representatives connected with the Kitsilano Local Area Planning Program,
the West Broadway Citizens Committee--a neighbourhood residents'
group which has recently ceased its association with the local area

planning program--and City Council, the final arbiters in most decisions regarding the future development of Kitsilano.

The interplay of these actors with respect to specific development-related issues is documented through the use of sources such as the minutes of local area planning board, public statements by representatives of the groups in question, and interviews with those representatives. The information thus derived is then analyzed with a view towards understanding the value positions of the actors, and outlining the areas of conflict and agreement in their positions. Finally, the importance to the emerging landscape of these postures is indicated via an examination of their role in decisions connected with the development issues under discussion.

G.W. Sutherland
GEOGRAPHY AND UNIVERSAL ORDER

An Introductory Course must incorporate an increasing number and variety of geographic specialisms and reconcile contrasting viewpoints. It seems to the writer that it therefore must have a single all-embracing theme, for while geography claims to integrate other disciplines, it must not fail to appear to be sufficiently integrated itself. Increasing complexity in both subject matter and technique calls for a core theme of increasing abstraction. The idea of geography as an ordering system is not new, but this statement on the concept of geography as universal order is a personal and perhaps individualized approach. It does not repudiate traditional geographic themes; rather it unites and complements them. It also permits the incorporation of modern philosophical ideas and appears to form a sound presuppositional basis from which the trends in current geographic research can be viewed, and from which the geographer can direct his attention to the articulation of the work of other disciplines. Confidence in such a core philosophical concept has changed the teaching of an Introductory Course from a distressingly fragmented and defensive experience to a unified, worth-while, and pleasurable one.

D. Gibson:

DIETARY REGIMES AND THE GEOGRAPHY OF DIET

The advocacy of geographic studies of diet is one of the chief characteristics, thus far, of the geography of diet. This area of study has long been characterized by the presentation of classificatory devices and schemes.

The reasons for the slow development of the geography of diet can perhaps be revealed by examining some of the problems involved in developing meaningful generalizations about dietary practices and patterns.

OCCASIONAL PAPERS IN GEOGRAPHY
WESTERN DIVISION, CANADIAN ASSOCIATION OF GEOGRAPHERS
(A refereed publication)

BRENTON M. BARR, EDITOR, The University of Calgary

EDITORIAL BOARD:

K. Denike, The University of British Columbia
M.C. Brown (Chairman), The University of Alberta
C. Crampton, Simon Fraser University
L. Evenden, Simon Fraser University
C.N. Forward, University of Victoria
P. Koroscil, Simon Fraser University
R.L. Monahan, Western Washington State College
I. Campbell, The University of Alberta

The Editorial Board assists with selection of manuscripts to be published in "Occasional Papers in Geography."

Papers presented at the Annual Meeting of the Division or at a meeting sponsored by the Division are eligible for publication in "Occasional Papers in Geography."

Sections Four and Five of the Western Division's publications policy state:

> An Editorial Board of not less than five persons shall be appointed by the Executive in consultation with the Editor. Board members shall be appointed for a three-year term, and after an initial period during which some persons have one- and two-year appointments, at least one position shall be filled with a new appointment each year.

> It shall be the responsibility of the Editorial Board to implement the Division's publications policy, to assist in selecting referees, to arbitrate in the case of a dispute between author-editor or between editor-referee, and to recommend the final contents of the volume to the Editor.

326
7325 x8